PREACHING
TRUTH
IN THE AGE OF
ALTERNATIVE
FACTS

PREACHING
TRUTH
IN THE AGE OF
ALTERNATIVE
FACTS

William Brosend

Abingdon Press™
Nashville

PREACHING TRUTH IN THE AGE OF ALTERNATIVE FACTS

Copyright © 2018 by Abingdon Press

This book is printed on acid-free paper.

Library of Congress Cataloging-in-Publication Data has been requested.

ISBN 978-1-5018-7024-8

18 19 20 21 22 23 24 25 26 27—10 9 8 7 6 5 4 3 2 1
MANUFACTURED IN THE UNITED STATES OF AMERICA

CONTENTS

ACKNOWLEDGMENTS

This work began as a presentation to a meeting of the Consortium of Endowed Episcopal Parishes, and was refined in a series of presentations to the clergy of the Episcopal Diocese of Massachusetts and at a conference celebrating the legacy of Fred B. Craddock held at the School of Theology, The University of the South. I owe thanks to all conveners and participants.

Brian Milford of the United Methodist Publishing House first encouraged me to explore how the presentations might become a book, a process through which Connie Stella guided me and Laurie Vaughen assisted. Thank you all, and to others at Abingdon Press who helped get the book out in record time.

Unlike my other books, *Preaching Truth in an Age of Alternative Facts* was written in a few concentrated months, without consultation with colleagues or obvious debt to mentors, teachers, and friends. Only my wife, Mary Ann Patterson, listened, commented, and loved me through the writing of these pages. This book is dedicated to her, with thanks and love.

INTRODUCTION

L onger ago than we remember, truth gave way to *truthiness*. Stephen Colbert re-coined the word *truthiness* on the first episode of his eponymous Comedy Central television show *The Colbert Report* on October 17, 2005.[1] Prior to Colbert's use, the word could already be found in the *Oxford English Dictionary*; but surely the American Dialect Society was right to honor *truthiness* as its Word of the Year for 2005. If only they knew what we know now.

Truthiness now seems to capture a bygone era of innocence and civility, with Colbert gently teasing Fox News' Bill O'Reilly as "Papa Bear." Colbert has moved to CBS, O'Reilly is banished from the network he helped build—at the cost of more than $25 million in settlement of sexual harassment lawsuits, and a similar amount to O'Reilly—but they have been replaced by legions of successors, if that is the right term. We live, work, politic, and preach in a time of fake news and, in the exquisite coinage of presidential advisor Kellyanne Conway, alternative facts.[2]

How are we to proclaim good news in the era of fake news? How are we to persuade others of the truth of the gospel when we live in a post-truth age? This is a challenge for which few preachers are prepared. And the strain is showing.

It feels like a tightrope. The pulpit is like a tightrope, stretched between red and blue, Republicans and Democrats, conservatives and liberals. And there is no net.

Everything I say is being interpreted and analyzed for things I never even thought about. Joshua and the battle of Jericho has become a commentary on whether or not we should build a wall on the border.

I cannot believe how angry people are.

It feels like I am speaking in someone else's code and I don't have a key to the code.

I'm old enough to remember when the big difference was whether you got your news from Walter Cronkite on CBS or Huntley/Brinkley on NBC. Now no one agrees on what constitutes news. Or facts.

I read the Beatitudes last Sunday and the tension in the church was palpable. Who knew "Blessed are the peacemakers" were fighting words?

Is this what it felt like to preach in the South during the days of the civil rights movement?

Try as I might I cannot help but tick somebody off. The gospel gets in the way of trying to keep everybody happy on Sunday morning.

Pins and needles. Or eggshells. Preaching is like walking on pins and needles on top of eggshells. I used to love to preach. Now I look at the readings for Sunday with my fingers crossed and hope there is nothing that someone will think is too political.

And on and on and on. In the classroom, at clergy gatherings and preaching conferences, and while chatting on Facebook or over coffee, skilled, seasoned, faithful preachers have struggled to gain their footing and find their voices since the election of 2016. In a lifetime of preaching and teaching I have never encountered this level of indecision and concern about *how* to preach. The concerns are multiple, naturally enough, and, while not confined to either side of the political spectrum, seem most pointed among those who identify with liberal and progressive politics. Understanding our rhetorical situation is crucial to imagining a faithful way forward. This introduction will therefore move from the situation, to the challenge, to the opportunities, and then to a sketch of the way forward that will be detailed in the chapters to follow.

THE HOMILETICAL AND RHETORICAL SITUATION

While there is little agreement on the nature of truth, most can agree that the current homiletical and rhetorical situation is one of profound distrust, surrounded by pockets of alienation. A growing threat of outright despair is leading to isolation and complete withdrawal from meaningful civic engagement.

Pilate's famous question in John 18:38, "What is truth?" (Gk. *Ti estin alētheia;*), is a clichéd but important place to begin, not just because it expresses how elusive the truth has long been, but because it does so with a cynicism that is central to the challenge facing preaching today. If there is a pattern to our conversation it is demonstratively downward in trajectory, from distrust, to cynicism, to alienation and disengagement. Homiletical intervention at any point must accept that the trajectory of the discourse trends away from trust, hope, and engagement and must respond appropriately.

Compounding the problem are listeners who express hope they can worship without hearing about politics. The assumption, of course, is that God, Jesus, and the Bible are apolitical, and it is the preacher who keeps bringing up current events and controversies. More than one parishioner has complained that if he wanted to hear about what is wrong with the world he could have stayed home and watched the Sunday morning talk shows like everybody else. The preacher may know that it was the biblical text that raised the issue, but that does not alter the complaint.

On the other side of the aisle the preacher hears from those whose complaint is completely opposite: why do you never talk about what is going on in the world? They missed last week's sermon on our responsibility to care for creation and thought this week's reference to Bryan Stephenson's book *Just Mercy*[3] was not pointed enough in calling into question the problems with our criminal justice and detention systems. You need to speak out more! The church should be the center of the resistance! Like the preacher above said, the pulpit is a tightrope.

The rhetorical situation, the broader culture of discourse into which the sermon is launched, hardly makes the task easier. There is simply no known precedent for the nasty and disingenuous nature of what passes for civic exchange today. Some pundits hearken back to the name-calling of early nineteenth-century presidential politics or the yellow journalism at the turn of the twentieth century. Nor was Jesus shy in his verbal assault on the scribes and Pharisees in Matthew 23. This writer has referred to the Epistle of Jude as twenty-six insults in search of a target.[4] So there is some biblical precedent. But the level of obscene, *ad hominem*, and demonizing rhetoric of those who in an earlier era would have been dialogue partners is, if not unique to our age, defining of it. On both sides of any given topic. There are no angels here.

To summarize the well-known: our rhetorical and homiletical situation is characterized by an almost complete lack of agreement on what constitute the facts of any given topic, so that truth remains ever elusive. Into that slipperiness is added a polarizing distrust of all who do not agree with our set of facts and our view of the truth and an absence of a shared granting of authority to any institution, expert, or text. All of it is exacerbated by a level of anger, accusation, and crudeness previously unknown in our society. How, for God's sake, can any preacher hope to gain a hearing by a church full of people when even preaching to the choir will likely pit the tenors against the sopranos? Welcome to the Sunday sermon in the age of alternative facts.

I checked. Preachers have been complaining about the impossibility of the task since Jonah. And just as no one, especially God, seemed to care how Jonah felt about the assignment, preachers get no sympathy, especially not from other preachers. Because we all know that no one is making us do this. We volunteered. Yes, God called, but only the most melodramatic among us pretend that *no* was not an option. If *no* wasn't a possibility, our *yes* was meaningless. We volunteered, full of optimism and passion, engaged and caring and ready to change lives and change the world. We had plans and ideas for innovative, cooperative ministry. We would help the hurting in all the ways we met them, whenever and wherever. We were not going to be chained to our desk, squandering our ministry in meetings instead of mission, in caretaking instead of outreach.

Remember?

THE HOMILETICAL CHALLENGE

In first courses on preaching, the student is introduced to the classic *V*-shaped sermon. First the preacher brings the listener down into the depths of sin and despair then pivots with the gospel to bring them home to heaven. Eugene Lowry's famous loop does much the same thing.[5] The challenge is to not bring the listeners any lower than the preacher has the capacity to lift them back up, to never dig a homiletical hole deeper than the preacher can climb out of. We face a similar challenge in talking about preaching today. Every preacher knows how hard it is and knows that the divides in the nation are also present in most congregations. This preacher is done reminding you.

Our task now is to appreciate the difficulties and begin to imagine a way past them. The challenge is to foster in our preaching and ecclesial life more broadly a place where genuine dialogue might happen, the pulpit as faithful alternative to the vituperative hysteria of pundits and prognosticators. This is easier said than done, but it can be done. Not by engaging the culture on its own terms; that has been tried by preachers who earned their fifteen minutes of fame by tossing F-bombs like comics on an HBO special. These preachers are now better known for losing their pulpits than for what they said in them. Instead preachers must follow St. Paul's still more excellent way and not the tongues of mortals and of angels (1 Cor 12:31–13:1).

There is abroad in the land the idea that conviction is evidenced by volume, and unless the speaker's face is red, arms are waving, and spittle is flying from the mouth, he or she is a mere *poseur*. The model of civic discourse is *The Jerry Springer Show*. And while it would help if everyone would calm down, it is essential that the preacher do so. Calm, confident conviction is what must be modeled in the pulpit, not attack-dog rabid hysteria.

Second in what might be considered this unilateral pulpit disarmament is laying down the rhetorical weapons so prominently used in broadcast and social media: ridicule, sarcasm, and the *ad hominem* demonization of those with whom we disagree. The pulpit often mimics the culture as a way of conveying that the preacher is aware, in touch, and gets the joke. This can be effective, for example when referencing popular movies and Netflix series, including the judicious sampling of film and music clips in the sermon for all to watch or hear. I am not advocating ignoring what is happening around us. But a great deal of what is currently popular is grounded on the humor of degradation. What began as put-down comedy in popular situation comedies (think Hawkeye versus Hot Lips and Frank in *M*A*S*H*) was honed to a fine degree in later years (*The Simpsons* and *South Park*) and is now not only accepted but also expected in many forms of comedy. Transfer this to political and civic dialogue and you end up with partisan news and political attack ads. Transfer this to the pulpit and another famous line from St. Paul, this time quoting Isaiah, is lost: "How beautiful are the feet of those who bring good news!" Here, Paul sings (Rom 10:15). But not if our feet are standing in a cesspool of disdain and degradation.

Simply put, if we cannot persuade without denigrating others, we are disgracing the gospel, not proclaiming it. Marshall McLuhan was right when noting a half-century ago that the medium is the message. As entertaining as it can be to make fun of the misunderstanding, confusion, or poorly formed opinions of others, doing so in the pulpit can both create the direct impression that such behavior is okay for the faithful, and leave a bad aftertaste that wonders if the preacher might not at times talk about the listeners this way. So, to again reference St. Paul, "When I was a child, I spoke like a child, I thought like a child, I reasoned like a child; when I became an adult, I put an end to childish ways" (1 Cor 13:11 NRSV). We will lose some cheap laughs, but humor at another's expense is unworthy of the pulpit.

Why is setting aside put-downs, sarcasm, and ridicule even a challenge? Because, along with snark, the rhetoric of denigration has thoroughly captured the mainstream of our society and has probably taken as prominent a place in your day-to-day speech as it has in mine. We do not even think about it. A few years ago I was challenged on this by a seminarian. My first reaction was defensive, and I argued that I was misunderstood. Then I watched a video of the sermon and had to admit that I sounded more like Jon Stewart than John Wesley, let alone Jesus.

Putting aside put-downs is easy compared to the principal rhetorical challenge of preaching truth in an age of alternative facts—not just staying positive but being persistently hopeful in our proclamation. This is much more than the challenge of making a good pivot in a *V*-shaped sermon or rounding the bend in Lowry's Loop. And it is more than recognizing that everyone within the sound of our voice has had more than enough discouragement this week.

Return to St. Paul, and to a passage we will consider more than once: "(We know) that suffering produces endurance, and endurance produces character, and character produces hope, and hope does not disappoint us" (Rom 5:3b-5a NRSV). Whoa! Or is it woe? Because the other thing everyone hearing our sermons has experienced is that hope gets disappointed all the time. Is Paul crazy? How can he claim that "hope does not disappoint us"? "Because," as he goes on, "God's love has been poured into our hearts through the Holy Spirit that has been given to us" (Rom 5:5b). It is not *human* hope we proclaim; it is the hope of God mediated by the Holy Spirit. The challenge is not to manufacture false hope but to consistently convey the hope that is ours through faith. While the "greatest of these is love," the thing in shortest supply today, and the thing the church is uniquely equipped to share, is deep and abiding hope. Such hope is founded on the love of Christ, not the vicissitudes of life. Never, ever forget that, preacher.

"Always be ready to make your defense to anyone who demands from you an accounting for the hope that is in you" (1 Pet 3:15 NRSV). Beautiful words, challenging assumption. More like, always be ready to dig as deep as you have to in order to find some hope worth defending. Hope, *elpis*; St. Paul says it abides with faith and love, *pistis* and *agapē*. Good company, and good to remember that hope does not abide alone but is found in community with faith and love, its own trinity—hope grounded on faith, reaching out in love.

THE OPPORTUNITY

If I have not ignored my own advice and dug a homiletical hole so discouraging you have already thrown this book out the window, let me point to the opportunity before us. We have an opportunity to model what is missing, and missed, in what passes for dialogue today—deep listening, real conversation, and honoring those with whom we disagree.

Among the many things we have learned in recent election cycles is that a large swath of the American public is convinced that their voices are not heard and valued by those elected to represent them and by the media that covers political, cultural, and civic life. If preachers ever risked polling the congregation to learn what they would like to hear sermons about, then compared the results to the subject of their sermons, they might find that their listeners feel similarly disenfranchised homiletically. That is a problem, but it is a problem with a solution: listening.

In *The Preaching of Jesus*, I argue that among the most prominent characteristics of the preaching and teaching of Jesus is its dialogical nature.[6] Whether in response to questions, in conversation with Torah, or because "he knew what they were thinking" (Luke 6:8), Jesus responded to the concerns of his listeners.

There are two very large lessons to be learned here. The first is that dialogical preaching does not mean we must have dialogue sermons to be responsive to the needs, questions, and concerns of those who hear our sermons, not that that may not be a good idea occasionally. However, a sermon without overt interruption or response can be eminently dialogical, provided the preacher has learned the second lesson: real listening is disciplined, intentional, and frequently frustrating. And it does not happen in the office. As hard as it is, as introverted as many of us are, we must put down the books, lock the office, and find some folks to listen to. And while you may start close to home, eventually you are going to make your way to those frightening folks we all say we wish would give our sermons a try, the unchurched. Gulp.

Here's the problem with the opportunity: to truly listen we have to set aside our agenda and discover what theirs might be. We have a conversation. Over time. With lots of people. Making sure they feel heard. Without saying, I think I hear you saying. It will not be a random survey of people from a database, asking them what's on their minds and what they would like to hear a sermon about. Nor does it have to be joining the Bishop of the Episcopal Diocese of Olympia, sitting on a barstool in Seattle watching the Mariners or Seahawks, while talking to whomever he lands next to about whatever comes up. Although that is a step in the right direction. It means, for most of us, rediscovering what it is like to have a parish and to be its vicar. Denominationalism, commuter churches, and cultural forces have blinded us to the neighborhood and its institutions, but most of us minister in a community. After talking during the coffee hour and to the adult forum crowd, the youth group, the session/council/vestry, the ushers and the altar guild—I know you, and this is where you will start—we have to hit the streets. The location makes this harder or easier, but the opportunity is always available. Get to know your neighbors. Get involved in their lives and their institutions. Work out at their gym and join their cycling club. Go to a reading at their bookstore, attend their ballgames, volunteer at their schools, go to their city council and school board meetings, and be a part of their community until it becomes your community. And listen. Out of these encounters and conversations will come the foundation for sermons that understand and respect differences and honor those differences without the kind of self-censorship that turns preaching into pabulum.

Over the years I have noticed that the students who fare the best in the first preaching course often have a background in high school and college debate. It helps that they have learned basic logic and so know what makes for a good argument. (Whether we think so or not, at its rhetorical heart, a sermon is an argument.) But it is perhaps more important that they had to learn the ins and outs of both sides of the position up for debate, not finding out until just before the individual debate begins whether they will argue for or against the proposition, and during the course of a longer debate contest eventually taking both sides. This does not mean the debaters do not have personal convictions on the topic; but they understand and respect each side. So must preachers. Making church a place where all people are honored and respected, even when we disagree—and yes, I hear you; I am not asking you to honor and respect hate, prejudice, bigotry, and the speech that supports them—making church a place of real dialogue is a great opportunity.

Who has time to listen, the preacher says. There is scripture to exegete, theology to outline, liturgy to plan, and that is just for one service, one Sunday.

Who doesn't have time to listen, the preacher answers. There is scripture to be heard, theology to reflect on, and liturgy to share, and that is just for this one service, this Sunday.

THE WAY FORWARD

If the situation is toxic, the challenge is to eschew the rhetorical weapons of the moment, and the opportunity is to invite, welcome, and practice active, engaged listening. Then the way forward is to ground our preaching in the conviction that biblical hope is not just a challenge to be sustained; it is the best response to cultural cynicism. It is what we have to give to the world. Our preaching must manufacture hope. Or more accurately, we must fabricate hope. Like Jesus. Fabrication is popularly understood to mean lying, but at its root means something much more substantial than telling a lie. To fabricate is to form and fashion something out of that which already exists, like an artist turning items rummaged from the recycle bin into a beautiful sculpture, or a storyteller turning the mechanics of first-century Palestinian farming into a parable of the kingdom of God. In an age of alternative facts, preachers need to fabricate hope out of the truth of scripture, the lives of their listeners, and the blessing of the Holy Spirit. There will be much more on this in chapters 4 and 5.

Shortly after the 2016 election I gave a talk on the topic that became the title of this book. The talk made six claims on the preacher:

You may be angry, but that does not make you a prophet.

Do you want to listen as much as you want to be heard?

They know how you voted. Do they know how much you care?

Have you laid a foundation for your words in your deeds and actions?

You must still ask the homiletical question: What does the Holy Spirit want the people of God to hear from these texts on this occasion?

When the time comes, speak your mind, not just your heart.

There was more than a little redundancy, which is helpful in an oral medium, but in written form those six points betrayed the ease with which the problem can be described and the difficulty in addressing the problem in ways that empower the preacher and the listener. Collectively the six claims focus on homiletical and pastoral humility, remembering that actions do speak eloquently, if not louder, than words, and reminding us that when the stakes are highest it is all the more important to be disciplined and ask the homiletical question.

In the chapters to follow we will answer Pilate's question and argue that in an age of alternative facts we must be clear on what the truth is, knowing that when others disagree at least we will be arguing about the interpretation of Scripture. Then we will focus on the characteristics of preaching in this season, making the case for preaching that is responsive, clear, creative, and convincing. One might ask how this is different than what preaching has always tried to be. It is not different, but in an age of alternative facts we need to be reminded of what that looks like and how to do it.

Well, I guess we will have to agree to disagree. You have your truth and I have mine. Really? That's the best we can do? It feels like giving up, moving on because it is too uncomfortable, too hard to listen to each other.

Then what do you suggest?

We keep talking. We keep listening.

TRUTH

O ne of the oddities of this season in our national life is that the word in the title of this book whose meaning is least clear is truth. How we arrived at this point was discussed in the introduction, and how we find our way forward is the concern of the chapters to follow. But without a shared understanding of the nature of truth there is no way forward, just a never-ending ride around and around on this vicious circle of a merry-go-round. This is not a work of epistemology but of homiletics. Nevertheless, Pilate's infamous question to Jesus in John 18:38 must be considered: "What is truth?"

Preachers do not need a philosophical or theological explication of the nature of truth, but a homiletical understanding of the nature of the truth we are called to proclaim. In other words, we do not need to make this any harder than it already is. Still, we might recall two classic understandings of the nature of truth because in a way the difference between these two approaches to truth helps us understand why truth has always been an endless topic of debate and is now a topic of such sharp dispute.

TWO WAYS OF VIEWING TRUTH

Whether one refers to them as an idealist versus pragmatic understanding, or "one group of philosophers" versus "another group of philosophers," there has long been a distinction between "coherence" views of the nature of truth and "correspondence" views. The former is arguably more theoretical, the latter more empirical, but that is just another set of distinctions to add to the mix.

The coherence view emphasizes that truth is best determined by how well the proposition in question coheres, or fits, with a larger set of propositions that form a complete system. In the most ideal sense a proposition is true only when it coheres with an inclusive understanding of all reality. The truth of a proposition is therefore determined by its coherence, or congruence, with an entire worldview. The view was expressed by modern philosophers, especially Leibniz and Hegel, and more recently by logical positivists.

The correspondence view adjudicates truth and falsity based on whether a proposition corresponds with what is observed to be the case. This is both logical (for something cannot both exist and not exist) and observational (we see, hear and feel precipitation, so it is raining). We may disagree over the form of precipitation; some might call it sleet, for example, but it is true to say that it is raining, sleeting, or snowing because we can observe the precipitation. This view goes back to Aristotle and is found in the much more contemporary work of Russell and Wittgenstein. It is also, frankly, common sense.

Even this small bit of epistemology can help us understand why our sermons sometimes founder on disagreements about the nature of truth. On the one hand, we preach from the foundation of a coherent system, the gospel, and adjudicate truth based on how well a claim works within that system. On the other hand, we also privilege a more commonsense approach within that system, while others do not. For example, an important proposition is that we are to "love one another." Few on Sunday will disagree, until we take that proposition to the border with Mexico and claim that prohibiting all immigration is inconsistent with Christ's command. A listener with a competing system will disagree, saying that it has nothing to do with Jesus but is about border security and the integrity of our democracy or about "stealing jobs from Americans." We are no longer arguing about facts; we are arguing about systems of coherence and how observable truths fit or clash with those systems. Preachers get frustrated when even the most basic "facts"—sometimes preserved for posterity in a video recording—are disputed. It will not help much, but it helps a little to remember that we are arguing not about facts but about the systems by which we make sense of our world.

In his monumental work, *A Secular Age*, Canadian philosopher and theologian Charles Taylor gives a persuasive account for how it is that in the last five hundred years we went from a world in which everyone, regardless of confession and creed, made sense of the world with some reference to God, to a world in which everyone, and again with no regard to confession and creed, makes sense of the world *without* reference to God.[1] Into this functional atheism creep many belief systems, and out of those systems emerge what Daniel Patrick Moynihan said we could not have: our own set of facts.

We see this when what for many are cold, hard, scientific data about warming temperatures and rising sea levels are, to others, just opinions, with which some scientist somewhere disagrees, so it is all relative. We are picking our truths based on what coheres with our systems, while pretending that we are operating with a correspondence theory of the nature of truth. I think.

3

What I am confident of is that the nature of truth is contested, and arguments about the facts are frustrating and circular. Put differently, we will no more easily convince in our sermons those who see the world differently than we do than we will in any other discourse. To do that we have to redefine the nature of truth, arguing biblically, not philosophically.

BIBLICAL TRUTH

We have to start somewhere, as a believer and as a preacher. Not our introduction to any particular sermon, but the starting point, the ground of our faith, and the source of any authority we may have as a preacher. We have to start somewhere. The choices are many: confession and creed; scripture, history, and tradition; testimony and witness. But before any of those options, in this season of our national life, we have to start with a clear and uncompromising understanding of and commitment to the truth, which requires a very un-postmodern understanding that truth is even possible. Not a construct, not relative, not a this-and-that; but it is an either/or, something that because it is, means other things are not. A belief that there is a truth to be known and proclaimed, debated, committed to, and defended. If this is old-fashioned, it is nevertheless the foundation of preaching. Before the incarnation, before the Trinity, before the creeds, comes truth. Believe it or not, but do not relativize it. Offer an alternative truth but not the possibility that opposites may both be true. When we agree that the truth is not just a possibility to be explored but a reality to be discovered and shared, then and only then can we answer Pilate's cynical question, "What is truth?"

Pilate's question about the nature of truth fits well into the theology of the Fourth Gospel but flounders on cynicisms in an age of alternative facts. The claims preachers make for the truth of the gospel is contested, and long has been, by denomination, sect, party, and tribe. As the Christian version of an older joke goes, every town needs two churches, the one I go to and the one I would not be caught dead in. And that is only to consider disagreements within the extended family of the faithful. In the ever-increasing number of those who no longer or may never self-identify as Christian, claiming to know "what is truth" is not simply talking about that which is contested; it is arguing for that which is widely denied.

TRUTH AS RIGHTEOUSNESS

My point is that thinking and speaking of truth only in terms of facts, propositions, and beliefs that one may or may not hold gives too much away at the outset. *Emet* and *alētheia*, the Hebrew and Greek terms for *truth*, are important biblical terms, but they are not nearly as important as *tsedeqah* and *dikaiosunē*, which are the words for righteousness. And while one hears often of truth as contested or disputed, the same is not true of righteousness. Because righteousness is not an opinion on data, to be agreed or disagreed with. Righteousness is a way of life. We best preach truth by emphasizing righteousness.

"I am the way, and the truth, and the life," Jesus said to Thomas, although we too often focus, for better or worse, on, "No one comes to the Father except through me" (John 14:6). Leaving aside exclusionary readings of the second sentence for another time, the first verse is essential for understanding how truth (*alētheia*) may best be proclaimed as righteousness (*dikaiosunē*). Because when Jesus speaks together of way, truth, and life, or when he earlier says in John, "you will know the truth, and the truth will make you free," after speaking of being "truly my disciples" if "you continue in my word" (8:31-32), the use of *aletheia* is expansive and is used to describe the nature of discipleship.

Is it possible that one of the ways forward is to stop arguing about the facts and start proclaiming the truth of the gospel is a practice, or set of practices, best captured by that very biblical word *righteousness*? If so, the standard for our "truth-worthiness" is not our accuracy, or whether our set of facts lines up well with the listeners' sets of facts, but whether our life in Christ commends ourselves to the listeners. Real ethos, not just rhetorical ethos.[2]

Among the questions in the lecture on which this book is based, mentioned in the introduction, is, "Have you laid a foundation for your words in your actions?" Are we living what we are asking for? Not that of the saints Francis and Clare, but *your* best life of discipleship. In seminary we run into candidates for ordination who misunderstand their role in profound ways, thinking that teaching is telling and preaching is telling loudly. Discipleship is what the pastor and priest instruct the candidates for baptism and confirmation how to do. Ordination confers some advanced status that releases one from the disciplines and practices of the Christian faith, or substitutes sermon, liturgy, and pastoral calls for study, prayer, and stewardship. You see where this is going. First to a confession, *mea culpa*. Then to a further reflection on the necessity to live the truth we proclaim, and to live it fully, faithfully, and well. Have you laid a foundation for your words in your actions?

I do not know anyone who understands herself to be a righteous person, and I suppose I would not trust anyone who did. Qohelet and Paul are clear on this one, "There is no righteous person, not even one" (Rom 3:10; cf. Eccl 7:20). But I know, admire, and seek to emulate people who are faithfully seeking after righteousness, who know what righteousness is and who show and share it every day in countless ways. Can we call them saints, or do we have to wait to do so until they have died?

How, preacher, do you understand the righteousness of God alive in the heart of a believer? What does that look like for you? Compassionate, accepting, forgiving, generous, courageous, and faithful are my words. What are yours? How we embody these practices—and that is what they are—matters more than what our list looks like. Have you laid a foundation for your words in your actions?

Pilate asked the question for the ages, Jesus answered it that afternoon, and God shouted his eternal affirmation of Jesus's answer on the third day.

Before we echo God's affirmation that Jesus is the way, the truth, and the life in our proclamation, before we seek to argue, persuade, and cajole in words, we have some things to work on. Because while no person is righteous, in the great divine paradox, "the righteous person will live on the basis of faith" (Gal 3:11; cf. Hab 2:4).

We proclaim the truth of the gospel by proclaiming and modeling faith and righteousness as best as we can.

LISTENING

The clearest message of the last national election is a deep and abiding sense of alienation from the electoral process, a distrust bordering on disgust of elected officials (although only in general, with high ratings for one's own representatives), and a constant refrain that the electorate feels it is not being heard. Nobody cares, nobody takes me seriously, and above all, nobody listens! This distrust of institutions and those who work in them and speak for them sounds familiar to students of history and to those who remember the 1960s, which arguably lasted from 1963 (The Beatles!) to 1974 (Watergate). And I know, if you remember the 1960s you were not there. I was nine, and I remember.

CRADDOCK WAS RIGHT

What preachers may remember is that out of the turbulence, this distrust of institutions and anyone over thirty, came the two most important books on preaching published in my lifetime: Fred Craddock's *As One without Authority* and *Overhearing the Gospel*.[1] The litany is well known: the civil rights movement, women's liberation, gay rights and anti-Vietnam War protests, all culminating in Watergate and the resignation of Richard Nixon.

Preachers struggled then, as they struggle now, to find their voices. And a then unknown preacher and teacher from a small Disciples of Christ seminary in Oklahoma had the wisdom and audacity to say it was time for preachers to turn to the listeners. It was time for preachers to stop asking, "What do I want to preach about this week?" and start asking, "What do I need to say to gain a hearing for the gospel, and how do I need to say it?" The turn to the listener was the heart of *As One without Authority*. The turn to indirection as a primary rhetorical strategy in response to the claim of Søren Kierkegaard that what is lacking cannot be communicated directly was the heart of *Overhearing the Gospel*. Preaching has been dealing with Craddock ever since. We will look at these intertwined claims, arguing for inductive preaching in an indirect mode, in chapter 4. In this chapter we need to consider a renewed turn to the listeners in our own age because our rhetorical situation is, while reminiscent of, markedly different than the one Craddock addressed forty years ago. Who are the people crying out to be heard? If we do indeed want to listen as much as we want to be heard, where should we start?

I noted in the introduction that most preachers will start with the people they know, the people they can count on, the people it is easy to contact. We naturally start close to home, but unless you have managed to select an unusual group of members at your church, some, but not all, of the diversity present in your community is present in your pews. So do not get too comfortable about the prospect of starting close to home. Provided you really do want to listen as much as you want to be heard. And this: people can tell the difference between a survey and a conversation; they know when we are just looking for support and encouragement and when we truly want to know what is on their minds.

It is church, so do not be surprised if many of the pews on Sunday include people who spent Saturday at a protest meeting or rally. I know it is church, but there are angry and frustrated people in the pews who are sick and tired of being ignored. They might provide a good place to start. Of course you may have to go to the rally on Saturday to do so. Or ask one of them to organize a listening group for you, ideally of those in your congregation and those who are not. Because the angry and frustrated want to be heard the answer will likely be *yes*. And while the intensity may be intimidating, there is one thing to remember about the angry and frustrated: they care. They are not frustrated and disengaged; they have not given up. They care, and they want to know if you care, too. As noted in the introduction, they know how you voted. Do they know how much you care? Caring enough to genuinely listen to their concerns, complaints, suggestions, and hopes is important, both to pastoral ministry writ large and to preaching in particular.

We need to acknowledge that many who hear our sermons are neither angry or frustrated, nor are so frustrated they are discouraged and disengaged. Instead they come to church to escape politics and problems. Other people are genuinely anxious and afraid, and while one might judge their attitudes to be exaggerated, their feelings cannot be dismissed. They, too, need to be heard because there is more than enough to be anxious about. However the stock market may be doing, economic insecurity is a genuine issue, the attacks on health care and other corners of the social safety net are real, and the threatened status of immigrant families touches many, many church families.

At the same time the fears of what may fairly, and definitely not pejoratively, be described as older, whiter parishioners cannot be dismissed by preachers who sincerely want to hear and not just be heard. They, too, need to experience that their pastor cares for them even though they know they did not vote for the same candidates last time. Or the time before that. One might dismiss their acceptance of a news story easily discredited by the facts, but as pointed out in the last chapter, it is inevitably a losing argument, made on the wrong terms from the start. Experienced preachers long ago learned that what most want is not to be agreed with but to know, to feel, that they have been truly heard. When that is what we want for our sermons how can we not do the same and listen carefully to our listeners?

THE UNINTERESTED, UNCONVINCED AND UNIMPRESSED

Some people are angry, others are frustrated, and still more are discouraged, anxious, and fearful. Has anyone been left out? Three groups have, at least we hope so: the uninterested, the unconvinced, and the unimpressed. We know the faithful will be there, though that is no reason not to be as disciplined in listening to them as we are to others. But we have to hope that our audience includes people who may not agree with our claims or who could care less about our perspective. On our best days, and often on the most important days of the liturgical and pastoral year, we will find ourselves preaching to the uninterested, the unconvinced, and the unimpressed; and if we are to preach to them effectively we have to find a way to listen to them as well.

The most difficult audience I have ever experienced or can imagine is an audience filled with people who could have cared less and were uninterested in what I had to say. To begin with they are perplexed by the very idea of one person standing up and talking and everyone else passively listening, perplexed because almost nowhere else in our culture does anything like this happen. Perhaps in a lecture by a struggling teacher who prays no one will interrupt with a question, or a politician who has been on the stump too long and has bored everyone, including staff, reporters, audience, and perhaps even himself, into a deep sleep. Outside of that the uninterested listener's experience is devoid of this rhetorical occasion, and if they are praying, it is in thanksgiving for their smart phone.

Why are they even in the pew? Usually because someone dragged them along or told them how much they would appreciate their coming to church before brunch or because the funeral or wedding was a family obligation. Whatever the reason, there they sit, mind drifting away, wondering what flavors of mimosa will be on offer after this nonsense is up and they can go to the restaurant. And yet, these are exactly the people we pray to find in the pew—young, smart, and more cynical and detached than is typical. They are the reason the preacher must work harder on the funeral or wedding homily than the sermon for the Sunday to follow. On most Sundays, unless it is an occasion like Easter or Mother's Day, there will be fewer people than at the funeral or wedding and certainly fewer unchurched listeners. Which is to say that if a preacher is deciding how to allocate scarce sermon preparation time this week, he or she should always prioritize the wedding or funeral homily. Not to boldly evangelize, but that by the quality of the sermon the preacher might gain the interest of those who thought they could care less. Miracles happen; they may come back.

The unconvinced can make up the most intriguing and receptive audience imaginable. They engage because they want to hear more, even if they are more akin to the Athenians in Acts 18 than a class of seminarians. With them the preacher is trying to make the case and persuade, not just trying to get their attention. The unconvinced took a course in religion and philosophy, realized that Narnia and the Shire were not just about lions and hobbits, and have some questions still unanswered. The funeral has forced questions of meaning and purpose, the wedding questions of commitment and relationship, and there is an opening, if not yet an openness, for the preacher to explore. Here it should be noted that a rhetorical strategy of indirection may well be off-putting, for the unconvinced want to hear what you have to say, consider it, and decide on the merits whether or not they think the preacher a fool.

The unimpressed naturally share some of the same attitude as the uninterested. Academic degrees, ecclesial titles, vestments, and attire mean nothing to them. Woe to the preacher who takes herself too seriously because this audience does not. Connecting with them requires an early and steady dose of what Aristotle in the *Rhetoric* called "ethos." Here ethos refers not to the moral character of the speaker but to whether the speaker appears in the speech/sermon to be a person worth listening to. As has been and will be noted again, pastoral ethos is shaped in the practice of ministry, and pastoral "capital" is gathered in that same practice. The pulpit is one of the places pastoral leaders spend some of that capital. In rhetoric, however, ethos refers to the observed character of the speaker, the audience's response to the appearance, posture, voice, and gestures. Preachers need both in order to come across as sincere and believable, even to the unimpressed. I am not arguing that preachers adopt a disingenuous persona, but that they do everything possible to let who they are—that is, a passionate lover of God and follower of Jesus Christ—be heard.

How does one begin to preach for an audience that we hope includes those who are uninterested, unconvinced, and unimpressed? These folks were not in view for Dr. Craddock, who admitted to an unwarranted optimism in assuming the very best intentions about everyone who stumbled into the pew. But there they are, pray God. By taking them seriously, listening to them, imagining and asking their questions, and doing so humbly and sincerely, connection is possible. What is needed in approaching all these varied groups of listeners is what I have elsewhere called "dialogical preaching."[2] Dialogical preaching is preaching turned toward the listeners, preaching that has learned to anticipate and answer their questions, even if the preacher remains the only one speaking.

Our very preparation for the role of pastoral leader and preacher may be one of the greatest obstacles to connecting with the uninterested, the unconvinced, and the unimpressed. Preachers have spent so much time answering the church's biblical and theological questions they have forgotten that the unchurched may have a very different set of questions on the same topics. While we are pontificating on the deutero-Pauline authorship of the Pastoral Epistles, they are wondering what an *epistle* is. While we worry about forgetting to get gluten-free bread for communion, they wonder why it smells like grape juice or cheap wine, what to do with the plate of money someone just passed to them, and if they will have to stand and say who they are before they can escape.

How does the preacher remember the basic human questions and respond to them without being patronizing or dismissing? It helps to remember just how much you had hoped someone like that would visit this Sunday. Then, in my experience, by asking a teenager for help, one who is clued into the culture, has moved on from Facebook and Twitter to the next new thing, and who is just as unimpressed with the preacher, perhaps by virtue of kinship, as the visitors may be. Preachers can too easily slide into asking questions of translation and tradition. The uninterested, unconvinced, and unimpressed are asking more fundamental questions, and in fact their questions may be more similar to the questions of most listeners than the questions the preacher is accustomed to asking or discussing among his clerical peers.

TAKING THE LISTENERS SERIOUSLY

Tom Long tells of an elderly woman who approached him and demanded, "You teach preaching at the seminary, don't you?" "Yes, I do," Long said. "Well, I have something that I want you to tell your students. Tell them to take me seriously."[3] It is easier, frankly, to take the listeners for granted, welcoming them along for the ride of course, but treating the sermon as a sharing of the preacher's personal encounter with scripture and the journey of faith. And so for many the operative homiletical question is, "What do I want to tell the people of God today?" Whatever that is, it is decidedly not dialogical. Recall Mark's summary at the end of his parable chapter, "With many such parables he spoke the word to them, as they were able to hear it" (Mark 4:33). Responsive, and responsible, preaching is focused on what is to be heard and shapes the speaking to foster the listening. Responding to differences in cognitive style and development is one way of taking the listeners seriously, and it is certainly in harmony with the model we see in the Synoptic Gospels. There is more, however. Long gets at this, as he reflects on what the woman meant in her demand to be taken seriously. "I have been thinking about what she said and what it might mean if those of us who preach genuinely take seriously the people who sit in the pews. I want to think, first, about what it means to take the listener seriously when the listener is not literally present; when we are in our studies doing biblical interpretation in preparation for preaching."[4]

If the greatest advantage and disadvantage the preacher has is that she is the only one in the room who has been thinking about the scripture lessons all week, one way to bridge the gap between the positive and the negative is to develop the discipline of keeping the listeners present throughout the interpretive and sermon-creation process. The ability to do so is why the best preaching, week in and out, is done in communities where the preacher and listeners know one another well. And Long is correct, in that it starts in the study, the first or second time you read the assigned or chosen lessons. At the beginning of the process we need to ask an entirely different set of critical questions along with the ones we learned in Old Testament and New Testament exegesis classes. Not "instead of" but "along with," for this is not in any way a suggestion to substitute rigorous, critical, scholarly work for asking what Aunt Sadie thinks about the book of Revelation. It is insistence that some of the important questions to ask of a biblical text do not come from commentaries; they come from the pew.

The discussion to follow in chapter 3 about bearing witness very much applies here as well. What are the life-shaking, gut-wrenching issues at work in the lives of the listeners? What topics have you consciously or unconsciously been avoiding, or danced around, in the hope of not exploding your church? Sounds good and makes sense, but how exactly does one preach dialogically, clearly, and persuasively? That is the focus of the chapters to follow, but first two kinds of preparatory listening are necessary.

GET OUT!

The first, hinted at above, is the hardest. You have to go and talk to people. As noted in the introduction, this is something of a back-to-the-future proposal to reclaim the idea of the parish as a geographical space, not a group of people gathered in a building. Yes, of course, you talk to the faithful, and you incorporate all that you learn from them into your preparations. But you cannot stop listening at the church door. A preacher is a member of a wider community, and the more deeply engaged with that community the preacher is, the more deeply her sermons will engage and connect with other members of the community. If a preacher limits herself to the folk on the church roll she will craft sermons designed only to speak to them. (That is the chime of the church's death toll you hear in the background.) If, however, she wants to reach out to, welcome, and include newcomers, she has to learn how to preach to them as well, and the only way to do that is to engage with them on their own turf.

Get involved. Go to meetings. Join something. Talk to strangers. And listen to them, to the sound of their lives and hopes and fears, to their questions, frustrations, opinions. How can the hope of the gospel be shared with those whom you hope will come for worship, and not just with those who do?

The second listening is imaginative. Knowing what you know about those in the pew and those you hope will join them, how do you imagine them responding to the scripture readings assigned or chosen for this Sunday? What do they likely not know that will help them understand the text? Where may they be resistant to the implicit claim of the reading, and where may they say, "Exactly!" when they hear it? Dialogical preaching means asking the questions of your listeners throughout the sermon preparation process so that the sermon responds to the listeners' questions, real and imagined. There is more to it than that, but it starts with showing that you want to listen as much as you want to be heard.

ONE EXAMPLE

An example might be helpful. Baptisms often draw newcomers, including the uninterested, unconvinced, and unimpressed, along with others who are there for the family of the baptized or are the friends of the one who is being baptized. They may be uncomfortably seated in the front, surrounded by people who seem to know what is going on, and they may be flanked by the gathered faithful who are excited to welcome new members into the body of Christ.

The preacher has a series of choices to make, including, in some traditions, the choice of what biblical texts will be read and what hymns, anthems, and prayers will be offered. Those choices will inform the sermon, if not define it, because different readings suggest different understandings of the meaning of baptism: dying and rising with Christ (Rom 6:1-11), following the example of our Lord and Savior (Mark 1:9-11; Matt 3:13-17; Luke 3:21-22), asking for repentance and offering forgiveness (Ezek 36:24-30), incorporating into the mystical body of the saints (Rev 7:9-17), and being welcomed into the household of faith (Acts 2:37-42), to name a few.

Reading the lessons the preacher asks the homiletical question, "What does the Holy Spirit want the people of God to hear from these texts on this occasion?" and it is the occasion—baptism—that jumps out. For church and guests, the preacher needs to talk about the meaning of baptism, why we do it, why we do it the way we do it, what it signifies in the life of the ones to be baptized, and what it signifies to the church. Here there is no question too fundamental to be asked; people want to know what in heaven is going on, be it infant, child, teen, or adult, be it a washing by the font or full immersion in the baptistry. Members need to be reminded, guests deserve an explanation. To connect, the preacher has to imagine their questions and answer them in a straightforward, unapologetic apologetic.

Explaining why we baptize the way we do is the easy part. Explaining why we baptize is the important part. And explaining it all in a way that welcomes and includes, rather than separates and excludes, is the hard part. And the best part. Explaining the stuff of worship is a vastly underutilized tool in connecting with unconnected audience members. I was raised in a tradition that practiced "believer's baptism" by full immersion. Now I live in a tradition of fonts and aspergillum. Oddly there is more water splashed about as an Anglican than as a Baptist. That probably needs to be explored in a sermon someday.

THE POWER OF LISTENING

Years ago, at a time that looked bleak to a political party that had been repudiated by the electorate for a second presidential election—with unexpected losses in the House and Senate—a conference was planned by a Washington faith-based organization with financial support from a midwestern foundation. Invited were members of congress and their senior staff. The conference/retreat was titled "Leading with Courage and Compassion," and the keynote speaker, who first gave a lecture at the Library of Congress and then led the retreat with the help of members of his monastic community, was the Vietnamese Buddhist monk Thich Nhat Hanh. It was as crazy and amazing as it sounds. Members of congress were doing walking meditation and listening to dharma talks and eating in silence. They were surrounded by practitioners from the Plum Village community in France, which is Thich Nhat Hanh's home while in exile from Vietnam because of his peacemaking activities.

Thây (Vietnamese for *teacher*) was in his prime and thoroughly unimpressed with his distinguished audience. He told them, in many different ways, that their power was not to be found in passing legislation, adopting budgets, or getting appropriations for the home district. Their power, he said, was in making sure that their constituents knew they were being heard. Their power was in listening.

That is also the power of preaching, which requires listening before speaking in order to gain a hearing for the gospel. Do you want to listen as much as you want to be heard?

Chapter Three

BEARING WITNESS

Preachers rarely hear, "That was a very brave sermon," after worship. "Thank you," "nice sermon," "good job," even, "I appreciated that very much." But, "that was a very brave sermon," is rarely heard. Why? To cut to the chase, what are we preachers afraid of? Short list: distracting from the primary purpose of the assembly—the worship of God, squelching dialogue, angering a significant donor, coming across as opinionated and taking sides, being seen as overly political. *Really* short list: getting fired.

There are good reasons to pull our punches, as the saying goes. To start with we have no business punching in the pulpit anyway. How does the old courtroom joke go? If the facts are on your side, pound the facts. If the law is on your side, pound the law. If neither the facts nor the law are on your side, pound the table. Same goes for the pulpit. We usually pound the pulpit when we are frustrated with the vacuity of our preaching. So let's be clear what we are talking about when we say that bearing witness is the first responsibility of the preacher in an age of alternative facts: it is not about real or manufactured anger, venting, blaming, or auditioning for cable news talk-fests. It is above all putting an end to voluntary self-censorship and sharing what is truly our answer to the homiletical question.

What does the Holy Spirit want the people of God to hear from these texts on this occasion? That is the truth we are called to proclaim. We will come back to it, but for now I want to use the homiletical question as a springboard to explore how the prophets can help us understand how to faithfully answer the question, remembering that the truth we preach is not relative, contested, or disputed but biblical, theological, and soteriological.

WHAT MAKES A PROPHET?

First, a lesson learned the hard way: just because you are mad, it doesn't mean you are a prophet. Most preachers have a story of how they learned this lesson, so I will not bore you with mine. (It was after Hurricane Katrina, and the rightly offended party never came back.) Getting excited, getting worked up, giving in to righteous indignation feels fabulous. Until it doesn't. Being angry does not make you a prophet. But what does make you a prophet? What does a prophet look like today, or, more to the point, what does prophetic preaching look like? Consider the following passage from Isaiah, on which this writer, at least, has never preached and never heard a sermon:

> In the year that Assyria's King Sargon sent his general to Ashdod, he fought against Ashdod and captured it. At that time the LORD had spoken through Isaiah, Amoz's son, "Go, take off the mourning clothes from your waist, and remove the shoes from your feet." And Isaiah did this, walking naked and barefoot. The LORD said, "Just as my servant Isaiah has walked naked and barefoot three years, as a sign and omen against Egypt and Cush, so will the king of Assyria lead the captives of Egypt and the exiles of Cush, both young and old, naked and barefoot, with buttocks bared, humiliating Egypt. They will be shattered and shamed because of Cush their hope, and because of Egypt their glory. On that day, those who live on this coast will say, 'Look at those in whom

we had hoped, to whom we fled for help and rescue from the king of Assyria. How then will we escape?'" (Isa 20:1-6)

Perhaps you have preached on naked Isaiah or at least heard such a sermon. It seems like a great opportunity for preachers who like to "become" a biblical character and preach his or her story in the first person. Naked preaching! Is that what prophetic preaching should look like? Pretty much. Which is why we do not hear it very often. Angry preaching? Sure. Preaching that blames, scapegoats, derides, and denounces? All too often. But truly prophetic preaching is about as rare as preachers standing nude in the pulpit. Because prophetic preaching is hard, disciplined, demanding work.

The work starts with recognizing that it is passion, not anger, that animates prophets and prophetic preaching. But, you say, righteous indignation flaring, even Jesus got angry. Yes, he did, but not when and where you probably think. (And we'll leave aside the fact that while I do not know you well, I do know you are not Jesus.) Most of us think Jesus got mad in the temple and tossed tables and drove out moneychangers as a result. But none of the evangelists say Jesus acted in anger, and in fact John and Mark suggest something very different:

In the temple he found people selling cattle, sheep, and doves, and the money changers seated at their tables. Making a whip of cords, he drove all of them out of the temple, both the sheep and the cattle. He also poured out the coins of the money changers and overturned their tables. He told those who were selling the doves, "Take these things out of here! Stop making my Father's house a marketplace!" His disciples remembered that it was written, "Zeal for your house will consume me" (John 2:14-17; cf. Ps. 69:9).

Zeal (Gk. *zēlos*), not anger. And how long does it take to "make a whip of cords"? I imagine Jesus sitting down, plaiting a whip while closely observing all that was going on around him and choosing the best way to make his statement.

The Gospel of Mark offers an even greater challenge to the "even Jesus got mad" crowd: "Jesus entered Jerusalem and went into the temple. After he looked around at everything, because it was already late in the evening, he returned to Bethany with the Twelve" (Mark 11:11). Jesus looked around and left. He slept on it and then came back and acted out in the temple a day later. Is that anger or a prophetic action?

To return to the Old Testament, were the oracles of the great eighth-century prophets—Amos, Hosea, Isaiah, and Micah—uttered in anger? The rhetoric argues otherwise. Isaiah said, "Come now, let us argue it out" (Isa 1:18), not "Go to hell!" Micah asked, "With what shall I come before the LORD, and bow myself before God on high?" and answered, "He has told you, O mortal, what is good; and what does the LORD require of you but to do justice, and to love kindness, and to walk humbly with your God?" (Mic 6:6a, 8). Hosea's marriage and family became a lived prophecy of faithlessness and forgiveness, and his oracles a call to, "Come, let us return to the LORD, for it is he who has torn, and he will heal us; he has struck down, and he will bind us up" (Hos 6:1). Who really thinks these beautiful, powerful words of Amos were tossed off in a moment of righteous indignation?

> Seek good and not evil,
>   that you may live;
>   and so the LORD, the God of heavenly forces,
>   will be with you just as you have said.
> Hate evil, love good,
>   and establish justice at the city gate.
> Perhaps the LORD God of heavenly forces
>   will be gracious to what is left of Joseph....
> Take away the noise of your songs;
>   I won't listen to the melody of your harps.

But let justice roll down like waters,
   and righteousness like an ever-flowing stream.
(Amos 5:14-15, 23-24)

We could go on through the centuries to Jeremiah and Second Isaiah, Joel and Zechariah. Petulant Jonah's story is set in the days of Nineveh— that is, the eighth century BCE—but is best read as a parable from a much later time and speaks of anger over a bush: "God said to Jonah, 'Is your anger about the shrub a good thing?' Jonah said, 'Yes, my anger is good—even to the point of death!'" (Jonah 4:9). Yes, my anger is good! Preachers know that feeling. But while many identify with fleeing to Tarshish, few of us claim this part of the Jonah story as a model for ministry. Claiming biblical prophets, up to and including Jesus, as justification for angry preaching simply does not stand up to inquiry.

Extra-biblical examples abound, from the Desert Ammas and Abbas to Francis and Clare, Eckhart and the Quaker tradition. The record indicates that more recent prophetic leaders, from Gandhi to King to Mandela, understood that speech and actions grounded in anger were counterproductive. Patience and persistence and courage and consistency marked who they were, what they did, and what they taught. Gandhi wrote:

> It is not that I do not get angry, I don't give vent to my anger. I cultivate the quality of patience as angerlessness, and generally speaking, I succeed. But I only control my anger when it comes. How I find it possible to control it would be a useless question, for it is a habit that everyone must cultivate and must succeed in forming by constant practice.[1]

If prophetic preaching is not founded on anger and indignation, what is the source of its power? Truth. It is the truth of God that, to recall chapter 1, is best understood as righteousness.

Returning to the eighth-century prophets, when Amos, Isaiah, and Micah contrast what seems to pass for conventional wisdom with what God wants from the people, it is not a change in attitude or opinion but a change in behavior and action. Amos, quoted above, and Micah's famous contrast between sacrifice, up to and including child sacrifice, with justice, love, and humility, is powerfully expressed by Isaiah in the very first chapter, setting the tone for all that is to follow:

> What should I think about all your sacrifices?
>   says the LORD....
> When you come to appear before me,
>   who asked this from you,
>   this trampling of my temple's courts?
> Stop bringing worthless offerings.
>   Your incense repulses me.
> New moon, sabbath, and the calling of an assembly—
>   I can't stand wickedness with celebration!...
> Wash! Be clean!
> Remove your ugly deeds from my sight.
>   Put an end to such evil;
>   learn to do good;
> Seek justice:
>   help the oppressed;
>   defend the orphan;
>   plead for the widow. (Isa 1:11-13, 16-17)

While we are conditioned to read this passage supersessionally—God rejecting the sacrificial system of the Jerusalem temple so, ta da! we Christians are in the right—that is to simultaneously distort the prophet's intent and give ourselves an undeserved pass. Do not confuse the form of the rhetoric, the rhetoric of contrast, with its substance, a call for all who believe in God to show their faith by learning to do good, seeking justice, rescuing the oppressed, defending the orphan, and pleading for the widow. To borrow from the rhetoric of another biblical author, we do not demonstrate the reality and depth of our faith by our words but in our actions: "Someone might claim, 'You have faith and I have action.' But how can I see your faith apart from your actions? Instead, I'll show you my faith by putting it into practice in faithful action" (Jas 2:18). I have elsewhere argued for reading James with Jesus, not Paul, as the appropriate conversation partner.[2] Here the claim is that faith, like truth, is about our way of life, not about our opinions.

One obvious challenge in preaching truth by emphasizing righteousness is that our listeners may be reluctant to join us in this move. But the alternative—to convince them to agree with us on a specific reading of the facts—poses even more hazards. An example may again be helpful.

TWO EXAMPLES ON STEWARDSHIP

The Revised Common Lectionary assigns Genesis 1:1–2:4, which is the first creation account, to two liturgical occasions when most preachers are looking almost anywhere else than to, "Be fruitful and multiply, and fill the earth and subdue it" (Gen 1:28): the Great Vigil of Easter and Trinity Sunday, Year A. (Those using the popular "creation lectionary" have another opportunity in the fall of Year B on the so-called Humanity Sunday.) That said, the topic of what it means to be a steward of creation knows few liturgical boundaries, and in the age of alternative facts, it can go very, very wrong.

Stewards! cries the preacher. That is what you are, for good or for ill, you are stewards. We all are caretakers of that which we did not create but was given to us by the goodness of God. The question is not whether you are a steward but what kind of steward you are going to be.

Right now there is a lot of confusion about what it means to be a good steward, which, frankly, I cannot understand. Scientists are as clear as they can be, at least the ones worth listening to. The earth is warming at an alarming rate, the ozone layer that protects us from the sun's harmful rays is depleted, and if someone doesn't do something pretty soon, Atlanta, Georgia, is going to have oceanfront property to sell, and all the major cities on both coasts will be underwater. Do you know what color polar bears are now? Brown! Because there is no ice in the Arctic.

Al Gore said it best, the time for argument is over; it is time for action. Exercising dominion over the earth means taking care of it, not polluting it. Coal-powered plants and gasoline-powered cars are killing us all. And that natural gas you think is so clean, do you know where it comes from? Fracking! Which is destroying the water table, making massive earthquakes in Oklahoma, and polluting aquifers so badly you can light what comes out of your faucet with a match and watch the explosion in some towns in Pennsylvania.

The time for argument, stewards, is over! I want to know what you intend to do about it and what this church can do together to stop global warming.

I imagine that might have felt pretty good to preach. I can also imagine that it backfired spectacularly. The approach to a contested topic was zealous, to be sure, but it was blindly so. Not only did it allow no room for disagreement, but also it seemed intentionally designed to antagonize anyone who might disagree with the preacher's reading of the facts. I am not by any stretch a climate-change denier, but I know that incendiary examples and controversial figures are as likely to alienate as to excite.

In another book I explored the homiletical question in some detail. So for now, consider a simpler question: what is the goal of a sermon on the stewardship of creation? Generally, it is to inspire the listeners to be more careful and committed in their consumption of the earth's resources and to think beyond gratification to consequences. If something like that is the goal, how is it best accomplished? Not by arguing in the sermon about the truth of global warming, but by talking about stewardship of creation as a spiritual practice, an embodiment of the righteousness of God the creator.

God (said another preacher), has in Scripture a tendency to say some truly outrageous things. "Be fruitful and multiply, and fill the earth and subdue it; and have dominion over the fish of the sea and over the birds of the air and over every living thing that moves upon the earth" is a good example (Gen 1:28). You are in charge here, to put it a little differently; take care of things. Take care of everything.

Wow. When did we volunteer for that? How are we supposed to take care of everything? Scholars and preachers have fastened on the words subdue and have dominion, arguing about their meaning and difference. Old Testament Hebrew likes to put words in pairs, however, and so to "subdue" and to have "dominion over" are not opposites but two aspects of what I more loosely translated as "taking care." Which brings us back to where we started—how are we supposed to take care of creation?

Noted Kentucky author and essayist Wendell Berry is known for having said, "Think globally; act locally," but he more often argued that we should both think and act locally. We need to be informed, paying attention to the guidance of specialists on climate, energy, and the best practices for protecting and renewing the earth. But unless we ourselves are one of those specialists, our energy and effort should be focused on what we can do, here, and not be consumed by debates about causes and effects. I am not saying to ignore those debates and leave policy to others. Instead, however you feel about climate science, as a steward we have responsibilities in our house, our backyard, and our community for the glorious gift God has given us.

Usually when the preacher starts talking about stewardship there is an instinct to reach for your wallet or purse. *Here it comes, I am supposed to give more.* Maybe, but this preacher is not interested in only getting you to give sacrificially of your income to the church. This preacher cares just as much about what you do with the *rest* of your wealth. Are you also generous without being spendthrift, careful but not miserly, spending within your means and saving for retirement? A steward of creation doesn't max out credit cards to drive a Maserati, nor does she or he hoard for the zombie apocalypse while turning down an invitation to go out with friends. Paul, of all people, got it right when he wrote to the believers in Rome, "Do not lag in zeal, be ardent in spirit, serve the Lord. Rejoice in hope, be patient in suffering, persevere in prayer. Contribute to the needs of the saints; extend hospitality to strangers" (Rom 12:11-13).

From here the preacher could move to tangible local examples, in the home and in the church, for the listeners to consider doing. Those examples should not be from the nightly news or the twitter-sphere but chosen from among the listeners themselves. There will be plenty to choose from. And of course, ask for permission first, even if the narrative is flattering.

The larger homiletical claim is that the most effective way to bear witness about the stewardship of creation is not to engage in an argument about the truth of climate science's warnings about global warming. Good topic for adult forum and the youth group, though. Because the goal of the sermon was not to win an argument about climate science but to motivate people to respond to the biblical command to care for creation. It is simply true that too many times preachers lose sight of the purpose of the sermon, that is, to persuade the listeners to live more fully as followers of Christ. In other words, truth as righteousness. End of example.

SOFTLY AND TENDERLY

Perhaps it is our love of the dramatic, exciting, even violent, but there is a tendency to focus on two aspects of the lives of biblical prophets: their calls and their conflicts and death. We read in the New Testament that "prophets are honored everywhere except in their own hometowns, among their relatives, and in their own households" (Mark 6:4) and that Jerusalem is "the city that kills the prophets and stones those who are sent to it" (Matt 23:37), but I cannot remember the biblical account of such a fate. Jeremiah comes close, of course, and Ezekiel's was not a bed of roses, but it is tradition, not scripture, that kills the Old Testament prophets. (I concede 1 Kings 18 as the Baalite exception that proves the Israelite rule.)

We remember the dramatic but quote something very different. Rarely does the preacher begin with, "Woe to you!" Is that because the preacher lacks the chutzpah to do so or because at its core the ministry of the prophet is not denunciation but invitation? Ask any Sunday school class what a prophet does, and after sorting through "tells the future" you quickly get to "speaks for God." The prophet speaks for God, in the Old Testament, often in the first person. And what does the prophet say? Usually one variation or another of "return to me," come back, and turn around. Again and again in the pages of the Old Testament the task of the prophet is to turn the hearts of the people back to God, to build bridges, and restore right relationship. A prophet brings the children of God home to God:

On that day I will answer, says the Lord.
I will answer the heavens
and they will answer the earth.
The earth will answer the corn, the new wine, and the fresh oil,
and they will answer Jezreel;
I will sow him for myself in the land;
and I will have compassion on No Compassion,
and I will say to Not My People, "You are my people";
and he will say, "You are my God." (Hos 2:21-23)

No, this is the covenant that I will make with the people of Israel after that time, declares the Lord. I will put my Instructions within them and engrave them on their hearts. I will be their God, and they will be my people. They will no longer need to teach each other to say, "Know the Lord!" because they will all know me, from the least of them to the greatest, declares the Lord; for I will forgive their wrongdoing and never again remember their sins. (Jer 31:33-34)

It would be easy to add quotations, and I do not deny that there are more than a few *Woe to you*'s in the prophetic repertoire as well. But even the *woes* are in service of the larger prophetic mission to bring the children of God home to God, to restoration—not simply to condemnation. The question for those who aspire to preach prophetically in our day is not how to be fiery and fierce, any more than it is a question of how to enter the pulpit as naked as Isaiah. The question is how to preach in a way that heals, restores, and fosters hope. To quote again from Isaiah, "You shall be called the repairer of the breach" (Isa 58:12).

Preaching with courage, in the manner of prophets old, new, and now, is not easy. It is not the substitution of volume for preparation, intensity for persuasiveness. Prophets have the courage to bridge gaps, not widen them, to invite dialogue, not shut it down. As my prayer book says at our baptism and confirmation, we shall "respect the dignity of every human being."[3] That includes the people whose politics differ from our own.

Prophetic preaching also requires that the preacher get it right. Our interpretation of scripture must be thoughtful and well-researched, our theological reflection must be rich and well-rounded, and our citations from any source whatsoever must be accurate every time. No "people are saying." You know what that means when an unhappy parishioner says something similar in your office. Nope, use names, dates, and exact quotations. Experience teaches that the more potentially controversial the topic, the more rigorous the preparation, and the more important it may be to use a manuscript that Sunday so that our words are tested and, if need be, tempered. A manuscript can protect us from ourselves.

Bearing witness projects confidence in demeanor, posture, and aspect; is measured in tone; and is dialogical in its engagement with the listeners. It anticipates and then responds to—not dismisses—the listeners' questions and their possible resistance to the claims of the sermon. It relies on the creative approach to the task we will examine in chapter 4, refusing to give in to the temptation to substitute emotion for persuasive argument.

The prerequisite to building bridges and repairing breaches is the holy, passionate desire to build bridges and repair breaches. To do so in our sermons is not a strategy for doing something else, such as changing minds or winning arguments, for example. It is the thing, the goal, and the purpose of our preaching: to (re)turn hearts to God, to (re)turn souls to Christ. The politicization of everything constantly tempts preachers to forget this. Which makes asking the homiletical question all the more essential. If we prayerfully and faithfully believe what we have prepared to say is what the Holy Spirit wants the people of God to hear, then we can and should preach with confidence, clarity, and conviction. We bear witness.

FALSE WITNESS

We must also take particular care that we do not bear false witness. While we have discussed the limits the current cultural situation has placed on claims to truth, narrowly understood in the sense of data, facts, theories, and opinions that are disputed in the service of various agendas, this does not mean preachers can themselves be careless or, worse, can actively participate in the transmission of inaccurate information for the sake of ideology.

That was abstract, so let me be clear. When you have reason to suspect that something may not be true, do not repeat it from the pulpit. When you have reason to suspect that something is being disseminated for ideological reasons, do not repeat it from the pulpit.

Let me be clearer: "Thou shalt not bear false witness against thy neighbor" (Exod 20:16 KJV). Among the neighbors we need to be especially concerned not to bear false witness against are those who have historically been the victims of discrimination, such as women, African Americans, Hispanic Latino/as, Asian and African immigrants, Muslims, and Jews. Even while we have learned to be more discerning and careful in many instances, we have an extra responsibility when bearing witness not to bear false witness.[4]

In the introduction, I argued for a rhetorical disarmament, putting aside snark and sarcasm as St. Paul put aside childish things. We must also eschew innuendo and the knowing wink, what in other settings has been denigrated as the dog whistle, audible to those who are in the know and get the joke. This is its own form of snobbery, and it undermines the integrity of sermon and preacher. It is also born of homiletical cowardice. Rather than naming directly, we use a snide reference, often known to rhetoricians as *metonymy,* mentioning a television network or form of social media, inviting the telling head nod of those in the know, while preserving what in another era was called plausible deniability if someone else took offense. Whatever this might be, it is not bearing witness.

A SERMON

If the preacher believes she has faithfully answered the homiletical question for these texts and this occasion, then do so with boldness. Talk about it, not around it. For instance, this is taken from a 2017 sermon on Matthew 22:15-22:

Does it matter who is Caesar? Maybe you remember—although it feels much, much longer, it was only a year ago—that, depending on your perspective, the president was a lying Muslim and Kenyan who had systematically and willfully been destroying our nation for eight long years. The American people voted for change, voted to "make American great (again)." Now, depending on your perspective, the president is a lying, narcissistic, delusional moron who is systematically cashing in on his office and surrounding himself with others who want to do the same. Depending on your perspective. Have I offended everyone?

You might wonder if there is somewhere in between? Of course there is. As Anglicans we seek the via media. Whatever your perspective is, things flipped last November, flipped upside down like a coin tossed high in the air. Does it matter who is Caesar?

Which brings us to Jesus. No stranger to controversy, at this point in the Gospel of Matthew, he has "cleansed" the temple and is now sitting in its shade, teaching, and answering any question those who do not believe in him, trust him, or want him anywhere near the temple can throw at him.

There is never any doubt that Jesus will "win" every argument. The only argument Jesus loses in the Gospels is with the Syro-Phoenician/Canaanite woman whose daughter is sick. Scholars have identified a common format to all these stories, calling them "controversy narratives," and in rhetoric, a challenge (riposte). Why does that matter, other than so I can show off? Because when you have a common format, any change or addition to the norm is interesting. In this case, the difference is not in the what, where, or why; it is in the "who." It is the Pharisees, sure, who have grown tired of losing arguments with Jesus over the interpretation of the Law, but they partner with the Herodians. The small, Jerusalem-based group of reformers begins teaming up with the Roman occupying forces. It is hard to come up with a fair analogy that is not too obscure, so I won't even try. It was a crazy partnership and illustration of politics making strange bedfellows, even in the first century.

Their simple question was loaded, once they got done with the flattery. It wasn't really about paying taxes, which usually came in the form of tolls and trade, so there was not much chance to avoid them. Then what was the question about? Loyalties? Resistance? Practicality? Realpolitik? Yes. All that and more. And as is so often the case, Jesus changed the terms of debate to suit his proclamation of the kingdom—and complicates matters for everyone.

You have to choose. There is really no via media here, nothing in between paying taxes and not paying taxes. There is plenty of room for interpreting the meaning of your choice, but you have to choose.

But choosing does not mean you stop being an outspoken practitioner of the Christian faith. Exactly the opposite. Rendering to Caesar does not mean you no longer take sides, nor does rendering to God. We take sides. Democrat, Republican, or somewhere in between, we take sides. One might preach about this passage as if deciding whether or not taxes will be paid—to Caesar or the IRS—settles everything. It doesn't; it just settles the tax thing, assuming you skip over the whole occupation issue and treat Rome and Washington as more or less the same.

As difficult as it might be, we pay taxes no matter who is in office, as an act of citizenship, for our common life and for the common good. We may get frustrated when many see taxes as something to avoid at all costs, but there are costs to government that someone has to pay. It is far better when we all do pay equally, according to wealth and income, but pay we will. And to this yellow dog Democrat, it is far, far better to do so as an act of duty, participation, and—dare I say it—patriotism.

The question for us is not whether to pay taxes but whether we can render to Caesar and render to God. Is it really either/or? Yes and no. The Apostle Paul meandered down this road in the thirteenth chapter of Romans, which are verses the lectionary prefers to ignore. He, like me, wants to have it both ways: "Pay to all what is due them—taxes to whom taxes are due, revenue to whom revenue is due, respect to whom respect is due, honor to whom honor is due." Clear, but he's not finished yet. "Owe no one anything, except to love one another; for the one who loves another has fulfilled the law" (Rom 13:7-8). You have to have it both ways.

Ken and Sally are like many couples these days, in that one votes Republican and the other votes Democrat, straight ticket. Their friends tease them that they might as well stay home on election day since they just cancel each other out. But they don't stay home. They never stay home. Because there is always something that needs to be done. And they do it together, whether it is tutoring at the school across town, spending one night a month at the shelter, raising funds for returning vets who are struggling with the transition stateside, or sitting on the board of the cooperative food pantry. You name it, and they are there. Nobody knows the extent to which they give of their time and money, and they might have the bumper sticker that reads, "We're spending our kids' inheritance." But they aren't spending it on themselves; they are giving to others, which is fine with their kids because that is the way they were raised.

We render to Caesar when we pay our taxes, go to the polls, and sing the national anthem. We also render to Caesar when we protest injustice, work for equality of education, pay, and opportunity, and welcome strangers to our shores, just as our grandparents and great-grandparents were welcomed in their day. We render to God when we remember that neither Caesar, the flag, nor anything else on earth is God. God is God, and Jesus is Lord.

Chapter Four

HOW

Among the many things students learn from the parables of Jesus is that content and form are inseparable. To reduce a parable to a meaning, historically a moral lesson, is to reduce the parable, making less of it than Jesus did when he spoke it. Sermons, likewise, cannot be reduced to a message captured in twenty-five words or less. Tom Long has taught us about the focus and function of a sermon,[1] but if a sermon can be reduced to a sentence or two, it was not a sermon worth preaching. Methodologically, however, we separate the what and how in our preparations. That is, we first determine a provisional answer to the homiletical question for the service at hand, and then we craft our way to the sermon that will allow the answer to be heard.

What does the Holy Spirit want the people of God to hear from these texts on this occasion? The question can be frustrating in the abstract but has proven useful in practice. In an age of alternative facts, this usefulness is heightened, for asking the homiletical question keeps the preacher from asking instead, "What do I want to talk about on Sunday?" In a season of conflict and controversy, of polarizing discourse and institutional distrusts, the last place the preacher wants to begin is with herself or himself. Instead we begin with prayer and Scripture, with the listeners and their needs, questions, and concerns, and with a deep appreciation that we preach not in a vacuum but in the midst of rich and transcendent liturgy and worship.

All of this has been recently surveyed and will not be repeated.[2] But the discipline behind any particular homiletic—be it that of Long, Buttrick, Wilson, Hogan, Craddock, Forbes, Proctor, Smith, or Allen, to mention a few of those whose methods have been invited into my classroom—must be emphasized. Preaching in an age of alternative facts demands rigorous discipline, and not just as the antidote to the wildly undisciplined rhetoric on the public stage and social media, as important as that is. Discipline grounds the craft in method, insuring that in a season when nothing less than the preacher's very best effort will do, that is what is being offered.

At its heart a sermon is an argument. The preacher is trying to convince the listener that this particular interpretation of a biblical passage, explanation of a theological principle, understanding of the contemporary situation, and proposed response to that interpretation, explanation, and understanding, is the most faithful. Successful arguments are logical, engaging, and compelling and rarely persuade by accident. Preachers must find the method most congenial for them and their situations, hone and perfect it, and be nimble enough to shift from one method to another as the occasion demands.

What the occasion this season in our national life demands was suggested in chapter 2 and must now be developed. I was tempted to title this chapter "Craddock Was Right" because I do believe that the way forward requires a renewed turn to the listener and that a narrative, indirect mode is called for to offset the bluster, bombast, and vituperation of contemporary discourse. But the late Fred Craddock has fallen out of fashion in homiletical circles. That is a luxury the homiletical guild can afford. But the preacher cannot. If, as already suggested, the closest analog to our age of alternative facts is the alienation and distrust of the 1960s, specifically from 1963 to 1974, preachers will do well to reread *As One without Authority* and *Overhearing the Gospel*.

Here's a question: Do you respect your listeners? In chapter 2 we explored how important it is to know your listeners, so that you are able to ask their questions, anticipate their objections, and offer the background needed to understand a biblical or theological claim central to the sermon. And I trust that you love your listeners, as you love all the people of God, while also knowing that a few of them may drive you to distraction. But do you respect your listeners? Do you value their opinions, acknowledge their wisdom, and trust their insights? Once upon a time the clergy were likely to be the only educated members of a community. Now? Rare is the congregation in which the preacher is even close to being the best educated person in the house. The congregation's wisdom may not be specifically biblical, theological, or liturgical, but unless it is truly respected, dialogical preaching is impossible, and condescension is a real possibility.

If one of the driving forces in this age is the widespread feeling that the public is not being heard, a preacher's capacity to truly, patiently, respectfully listen to her parishioners is vital. In turning to the listeners, and turning away from cynicism, sarcasm, and the denigration and dismissal of difference, the preacher is able to also turn toward authenticity, integrity, and trust. It is always and only a two-way street. Do you want to listen as much as you want to be heard?

But what if what they know is not true, what they believe is mistaken, and their opinions are dangerously misguided? Must the preacher still respect the listeners and their insights? Yes. Because there is no hope of persuasion in an atmosphere of disrespect. Recall the aftermath of the 2016 election, when pundits were pointing to one party's inability to understand and connect

41

with a significant portion of the electorate as the reason for the results. There is no reason to be more specific, because in the next election the tables will as likely as not be turned, while the finger-pointing continues. Politically the logistical calculation was whether it was better to use limited resources to motivate the base to get out and vote or to commit significant resources to reaching out to others who had historically not been supportive. This is a calculation preachers do not have the luxury of making. Preachers who pitch their sermons for the listeners who share their biblical, theological, social, and political opinions will soon be preaching only to themselves. Good preachers, in whatever age, do not focus on election cycles or news cycles; good preachers take the long view. God's view. This does not mean ignoring the news or an upcoming election; it means not focusing on it.

THE LONG VIEW

Like it or not, pastoral leaders spend their ministries teaching something they were not planning on and for which they may not have prepared adequately. Like it or not, we teach hermeneutics—not only how to interpret scripture, theology, and ethics, but also how to interpret situations.[3] This is not something accomplished in a single Sunday sermon. It happens over the lifetime of the preacher's relationship with a congregation. Woe to the preacher who dares to challenge every unexamined assumption and deeply held conviction present in the parish on her first Sunday. And woe to the preacher who departs to greener pastures years later never having done so. If you cannot say some things in your fifth year that you could not say in your first year then you have been wasting four years.

Most preachers know instinctively that this is true when introducing historical-critical exegesis to a beloved passage of scripture or offering a new reading of the doctrine of the atonement. Here we easily take the long view, preparing church members through classes, readings, guest speakers, and sermons. Why would we approach a controversial social or political topic any differently? For instance, while in many cases there are no ecclesial or hierarchical barriers to the advancement of women in ministry, in practice the barriers are immense and the stained-glass ceiling impenetrable. The same is true for persons of color, members of the LGBTQ community, and those who are differently abled. Passing resolutions at church conventions can help but not nearly as much as the pastoral leader who intentionally and systematically welcomes women, African Americans, LGBTQ persons, Hispanics, and someone in a wheelchair to places of leadership and visibility in the church, such as guest preacher or retreat leader and so on. Similarly, by using illustrative material—stories, historical examples, analogies, and comparisons—that feature persons whose appearance differs from congregational expectations, those expectations are gradually shifted. In this way the privileged pastoral leader can prepare the way for the church to welcome someone as his successor they would never have considered a few years ago.

And here, of course, is the problem. We don't have a few years. The crisis is now. Yes, it is, but the answer still requires taking the long view. God's view. We must earn trust before we change minds, show them how much we care before we tell them how we voted (they already know how you voted, by the way), and lay the foundation for our words in our actions. And express and explain over time the biblical, theological, and ethical foundation for our convictions and for the actions that those convictions demand. Even in an age of alternative facts we are still called to make disciples, after all.

How we preach in this age requires that we focus on gaining a hearing for the gospel by focusing on the listeners and by planning and preaching on a longer homiletical horizon than this Sunday. Real and meaningful changes in attitude that lead to changes in action, often reported to be immediate and surprising (Acts 9), actually take time, determination, and stubborn commitment (Gal 2). How we preach in this age also calls for a strategy of indirection, supported by a rhetoric that is persistently figurative.

"There is no lack of information in a Christian land," Craddock famously quoted Kierkegaard to launch the Beecher Lectures published as *Overhearing the Gospel*. "Something else is lacking, and this is a something which the one (person) cannot directly communicate to the other."[4] We may still argue about whether this is a "Christian land" and draw conclusions about biblical illiteracy, but two things abide: there is no lack of information, real and fake, and the something lacking cannot be communicated directly. I doubt it ever could.

Shut up!
Get outta my face!
Who do you think you are?
I said shut the *%#& up!
I don't have to listen to this bull#@$!
Shut up!

Or words to that effect. In my memory shouting pundits go back to William F. Buckley's *Firing Line* and Dan Ackroyd and Jane Curtin's parody of *60 Minutes's* "Point/Counterpoint" on *Saturday Night Live*, though it may go back to Origen's *Contra Celsum*. In any case as the years have gone by, the language has grown coarser, the *ad hominem* attacks have become more frequent and more pointed, and the message has become loud and clear, or at least loud. Popular and social media provide no models for preaching truth in an age of alternative facts. Our models are biblical, the *meshalim* of the Old Testament prophets, and the parables, allegories, metaphors, analogies, and hyperboles (all species of the genus *mashal*) of Jesus.

Let's agree that the facts are on our side. All of the data, all of the peer-reviewed articles, all of the evidence and statistics support the position we plan to take in the sermon. It does not matter unless the information, the facts, the truth, can be conveyed as a part of a compelling narrative. Unless we have a compelling story, within which all our stories can find room, all of the information in this land, Christian or not, will not persuade. Fortunately we have as our exemplar the very word of God incarnate, Jesus, whose parables are without peer or parallel.[5]

Now is not the occasion to explore the parables of Jesus but to focus on three aspects of the parables that have particular resonance for this homiletical season: the importance of story, the capacity of those stories to create worlds anew, and the enduring hope these short stories have sustained. Together these three suggest how we are to preach truth in an age of alternative facts.

NARRATIVE PREACHING

This is no more a work on narrative theory than it is a work of epistemology. So we will not engage debates about narrative preaching and narratives in preaching. For what one first notices is that those who describe the decline of narrative in preaching use anecdotes to make the case. How could they do otherwise? One need not make a claim for humans as *homo narrationis* to note that we seem to enjoy stories. A lot. Preachers have long tapped into this, though none with the success of Jesus. I have previously argued that if our preaching about Jesus looked more like the preaching of Jesus as recorded in the Gospels our proclamation might be more effective.[6] Here the claim is a little different, emphasizing the indirect communication that takes place when sharing a story. It is what our English composition teacher told us years ago. Don't *tell* them, *show* them. In this season, when listeners are bombarded with people telling them what to think, who to believe, and how to vote, the preacher who steps back, slows down, and shows them in a story what she would like them to consider will be much more likely to gain a hearing for the gospel.

Where is the preacher to find such stories? That seems like a ridiculous question in an age of alternative facts. Just use Google, YouTube, or Facebook. My late father, a Baptist preacher, had a thick book titled *McCartney's Illustrations*. The stories and anecdotes were organized alphabetically. If you wanted a story about "forgiveness" you simply flipped to the "f's." Now you can do a Google search. I just did. "Forgiveness" yielded 43,400,000 hits. Hmm.

Preachers do better to start with their own lives and experiences. You have a life, don't you? You read, watch, listen, walk, and wonder; you came from and have a family, friends, and an education. All of this provides the material for stories, almost none of which need be in the first-person singular unless you have some compelling reason to do so.

In an age of alternative facts this part is going to get tricky, so bear with me. Because finally I am asking you to do what Jesus did; that is, create your own stories. In earlier times I referred to this as "WWJD: make stuff up. We call them the parables." But in this age encouraging preachers to "make stuff up" just might be misunderstood. So I invite you to think of yourself as a storyteller, in the tradition of Jesus, who drew on experience and observation to craft stories whose meaning reverberated in the lives of his listeners.

Why tell stories in an age of alternative facts? Because stories are disarming, persuasive, and memorable. "You know what's wrong with you?" Yes, you have the listeners' attention, but you also have their defenses up, and they are much more likely to resent and resist than listen and learn. If instead you try to show them what the problem might be in the form of a story, there is an excellent chance they will find themselves agreeing with you without ever imagining you have them in mind. "Two men went up to the temple to pray," Jesus begins in Luke 18:10. By the time they come down from the temple mount, the listeners have been implicitly invited to make an untenable choice: am I like the forgiven tax collector or the Pharisee who has nothing for which he needs to be forgiven? Gotcha! But it is a double gotcha. While neither character comes across as especially worthy of our respect or emulation, on the best reading of the story both of them go home "having been made righteous" (my translation).

Which brings us to the second reason stories are especially effective in our sermons today: through them the preacher creates the world in which faith is seen and imagined. Jesus created a world by saying, "There was a rich man" (Luke 16:1), or, "A man...had two sons" (Luke 15:11). We are accustomed to, "Once upon a time" and "It was a quiet week in Lake Woebegone." What about a world of faith? Of faithful service? Of generosity, compassion, and forgiveness? Preachers can make that world, two minutes at a time. All you need is already at hand—character(s), plot, and conclusion—and because the preacher is the storyteller, the trajectory of the story is shaped to fit the need of the sermon. There is more than enough discouragement, despair, and anguish in a ten-minute news summary to depress a congregation of five hundred souls for a week or two. They do not need to be told that, to quote a local construction worker, "dark times are comin'." They know dark times are here.

If one more thing goes wrong I will scream, she thought. It did, and she didn't; but she wanted to. It's always something, she thought, as she packed her violin beside the cooler packed with sandwiches, fruit, and water. What did they call themselves, only kidding a little bit? "The down and out quartet." For musicians they were anything but—conservatory-trained members of the symphony, with as many students on the side as they wanted. And just about every Monday the four of them headed somewhere, a prison, a rehab center, a school, or like today, four chairs in a park where they would play Beethoven and Radiohead, and share their sandwiches and music with the homeless. Why did they do it? Because you give what you have, and they have music. Along the way they've met a surprising number of talented singers and players, and they have found used instruments to share, given a few free lessons. They have talked about having a concert to raise money and awareness, featuring these talented, homeless, struggling, wonderful folk. Because you give what you have, and what they have is music.[7]

Stories create worlds, and the preacher who creates stories decides what the world looks like that day, in that sermon. The question is not whether the story is a faithful re-creation of an observed event but whether it is faithful to the gospel and helpful in answering the homiletical question. Nobody asked Jesus whether the story of the good Samaritan really happened. To do so is to misunderstand the nature of the parables. You're no Jesus, but you can learn to fashion compelling, gospel-infused stories. Like all craft it takes practice; Malcolm Gladwell was not kidding about the 10,000 hours.[8]

The last thing to say about the use of stories in sermons is that they can become a factory, in particular, a factory of hope. Paul writes, apparently without irony, that "suffering produces endurance, and endurance produces character, and character produces hope, and hope does not disappoint us, because God's love has been poured into our hearts through the Holy Spirit that has been given to us" (Rom 5:3b-5 NRSV). We are preaching to people who know damn well that hope disappoints, and disappoints all the time. Then what is Paul talking about as he climbs this ladder of hope? Simply put, he is redefining hope, defining it theologically, perhaps a little eschatologically, creating a world in which *God's* hope does not disappoint, because *God's* love and *God's* Spirit have been poured into our hearts.

It is quite a claim, and the truth of it is put to the test every time we preach. Can we engender hope this week? Can our sermon be a part of the church's efforts to engender hope this week? Can we, through story, imagine ways to overcome the impasse and division undermining our national life? Preachers of a certain age will remember Operation Push, and its founder and longtime leader, the Rev. Jesse Jackson. Jackson is known for many things, not all of them positive. There were the shouts of "Run, Jesse, run!" which encouraged him to run for the presidency or to get out of town, depending on the shouter. There was the time he (rightly) claimed that if he were to walk on water the press would report, "Jesse can't swim." But in my memory he will always be treasured for the motto and mantra of Operation Push: *Keep hope alive!*

Keep hope alive! That almost sounds like a job description. Little need be added except to reemphasize how important it is, and how easy it is to watch as frustration, cynicism, and despair push hope aside. Preachers are not bystanders, however. Preachers intervene, creating worlds of hope in which listeners can imagine themselves living rightly and faithfully and imagine their church being a change agent, a "hope factory," in their community. The key of course is for the preacher to be genuinely hopeful. This is grace, to be sure, but it is far from impossible. It happens every Sunday, thousands of times.

One of the national divides most directly impacting the life of the church has to do, variously, with the free exercise of religion. Must I bake your wedding cake if I do not approve of same-sex marriage? Am I required to offer contraception in my company health insurance policy if I think contraception ends a life by preventing fertilization? These are contentious issues, resolved not in church but in the Supreme Court. Preachers are well aware that much more is at stake than wedding cakes and condoms and that the "free exercise" claim cuts both ways. What we do not hear is mention of Jesus's admonishment to settle with the accuser rather than go before the judge, James's admonishment not to favor the rich who take members of the community to court, and Paul's admonishment in Romans 14 and 15 that those who are strong must take particular care not to offend the weak. Simply put, those who seek legal relief or support for their positions do so without biblical precedent.

But that will not preach, at least not directly, any more than constructing an ethic of cake baking will help one preach on the complex and multiple issues of contemporary sexuality. However, imagining how one might bring the New Testament's apparent dis-ease with the legal system to bear on areas of disagreement within the community, while also exploring the responsibilities that come with having strong opinions on controversial topics, could be effective.

Alex was frustrated. She gets that way when she does not understand, and she did not understand Joellen at all. What was she talking about? Joellen wasn't gay, none of their friends were. Why did she suddenly start caring about gay rights? "Rights are rights; if they start taking rights away from one group, you might be next." She sounded like a bumper sticker. Rights are rights? What about my right not to be annoyed by you and your rights? That's when Joellen sounded like she was mad, talking about how those of us who have everything in our favor have to let go of some of our power and privilege so others have a chance. Where does she get that stuff? She said it was in the Bible but she didn't say where. Like I was supposed to know.

References to Matthew 5:25-26, James 2, and Romans 14–15, among other passages, help bolster but do not make the argument, any more than the most recent polling data or scientific evidence will convince someone who sees the world differently than the preacher does. The sermon's task is to persuade, not to prove.

Which reminds us that our working understanding of truth is not verifiable, peer-reviewed, replicable data; our way forward is understanding truth as righteousness. In the examples above, cakes and condoms, which is the path of righteousness? I am intentionally forcing the term in an unfamiliar way. We are accustomed to hearing the word *righteous* and thinking puritanical, rule-bound, unforgiving. But that is not *tsedeqah* and *dikaiosunē*, nor is it the Old Testament prophets and the prophet Jesus. Righteousness is the full, embodied, messy, and complicated way of discipleship. The righteous will live by faith, and the faithful will live by righteousness. Preachers have to show what that looks like.

A friend on the border says the wall is for people who live at least five hundred miles from Mexico. In El Paso it is just an inconvenience. On Sunday morning in his church the visitors are asked to stand, share their name, and say where they were from. They were from Ciudad de Juarez, crossing the border to go to church. On Monday they will come back and find work in the parking lot of Home Depot or be picked up in another spot he showed me for their jobs as nannies, cooks, cleaners, and gardeners. It is the way of the border. Build a sixteen-foot wall, we'll get eighteen-foot ladders, he joked. Then he took me up to the pass that gives the city its name. When you look down you cannot see a border, because the pass is the border; at least it is the border nature intended. Down there, where even the river is lined in cement, there are just jobs to be done and people to do them.

A SERMON FOR PALM/ PASSION SUNDAY MARK 14:32–15:39

We have just heard a long, sad story with a familiar, tragic ending. Marcus Borg and Dominic Crossan argue that the liturgical recovery of Passion Sunday is necessary because so few of us will return to worship this week on Maundy Thursday or Good Friday. So if we don't read the Passion gospel now we skip too easily from Hosanna to Alleluia.[9] Point taken.

What shall we make of this story, on this day, calling us to sharp reflection at the beginning of Holy Week? Every time I read it something different catches my thought, but one verse, again and again, year after year, will not leave me alone. Mark 14:50, "And all his disciples left him and ran away."

In the Revised Standard Version of my upbringing and education the verse reads, "And all forsook him, and fled." As Mark tells the story this abandonment is startling, striking. The disciples, led by impetuous Peter, pledge at supper to stand and die with Jesus. Their "stand" consists of one swipe at a servant's ear, then away into the night. We do not know where they go, save for Peter who goes to the courtyard and a handful of women who go to the cross. While the Cyrenian may carry the cross for a time, in the most profound way imaginable, Jesus walks the Via Dolorosa and dies on Golgotha, abandoned and alone. What form does our abandonment take?

I think most of us know ourselves well enough to realize we would do much the same. The truth is, we do it now, every day. Jesus comes, proclaiming the gospel of God (Mark 1:15), and we flee, flee to our private, personal faith, turning our backs on others and on the community it takes to build and sustain the kingdom of God.

Jesus comes, curing "many who were sick with various diseases, and cast[ing] out many demons" (Mark 1:34 NRSV), and we flee, flee from the messiness and sadness of illness and suffering, assuring ourselves that our health care system is second to none, give or take the tens of millions of our fellow citizens still without health insurance, and a focus on prescription solutions that overlooks the prevention that might keep us from illness in the first place.

Jesus comes, and "taking the five loaves and the two fish, he looked up to heaven, and blessed and broke the loaves, and gave them to his disciples to set before the people; and he divided the two fish among them all. And all ate and were filled" (Mark 6:41-42). We flee, safe in the knowledge that we will "always have the poor . . . , and [we] can show kindness to them whenever [we] wish" (Mark 14:7), confident that one day we will in fact wish to help the poor.

Jesus comes, teaching "as one having authority" (Mark 1:22), teaching us to love the Lord with heart and soul and mind and strength and our neighbors as ourselves (Mark 12:30-31), and we flee, flee to silly questions about the identity of our neighbors and to the sad truth that we do not even know our neighbors' names.

Our abandonment takes many forms—denial, ignorance, willfulness, fear, dependency, and selfishness. Like the young man in the linen tunic, when we run away, we run away naked. It may be dark, so no one notices. But we know. God knows.

We flee, to the intensely personal, protected, and pious. Jesus's execution was public, brutal, and political. All of our well-intended, if ultimately barbaric and futile, theories and theologies of the atonement stumble on this: Jesus did not die for our sins. To say "Jesus died for our sins" sounds like he passed away in his sleep at a ripe old age and remembered us in his will. Jesus did not die; he was killed, by an efficient, violent, occupying power and its local collaborators. We read in a favorite Collect at Morning Prayer that Jesus "stretched out his arms of love on the hard wood of the cross that everyone might come within the reach of (his) saving embrace."[10] And we read in Eucharistic Prayer A, "He stretched out his arms upon the cross, and offered himself, in obedience to your will, a perfect sacrifice for the whole world."[11]

Beautiful words. Historical nonsense. Jesus's arms were stretched out on the cross by Roman soldiers, who held his hands and feet in place while spikes were driven into his ankles and wrists. Jesus did not die for us. Jesus lived for us, fully, faithfully, passionately. And we killed him for it.

Is abandonment inevitable? Is that what it means to take up our own cross—that we leave Jesus to go to his cross alone? That is the question for this Holy Week. It is a personal question, and a question for this and every church. What would it look like for you and me to decide, this week, not to run with the disciples but to follow with the women, with Mary Magdalene, Mary, "the mother of Joses" (Mark 15:47)—which is Markan code for Our Lady—and Salome?

Certainly it means not to run from the story but to "read, mark, learn, and inwardly digest" the story, to borrow from another Collect. Set aside time this week to read the first fifteen chapters of the Gospel of Mark. It will take about an hour. Slow down when you come again to chapter 14. Walk with Jesus.

Recalling the story is important. Living faithfully in response to the story is discipleship. It is a very political story, with very political implications. Christian faith, rightly understood and practiced, is a way of life in community, not a personal, private set of opinions. Following the women to the cross is feeding the hungry, ministering to the sick, remembering the lonely, encouraging the distressed, and telling the story, your story, of faith, with all its stumbles, all its hopes.

In the chapel of Cathedral College in Washington, D.C., is a crucifix unlike any I have ever seen. Jesus, on the cross, does not have his arms stretched out. His arms enfold someone, someone small, unremarkable, unrecognizable. If you look closely, you will see who he holds on the cross. It is you. It is me.

SOME SUGGESTIONS

We have argued that arguing about facts is a losing argument every time. We will not convince our listeners who deny climate change, fear the impact of immigration, and are sure most recipients use food stamps to buy filets and lobster tails at Whole Foods that it is their sources purveying fake news. Instead preachers need to be biblical in their rhetoric, echoing prophets from Isaiah to Jesus, and talk about truth as righteousness, using images and examples of faithful discipleship, not data points, as our evidence. This evidence grows out of our sincere and tireless listening to the lives of others and our commitment to being, regardless of denomination, the vicar of the parish, fully engaged and involved in the life of our community. To this community, inside and beyond the church doors, we bear witness and give testimony to the good news of Jesus Christ, having patiently laid a foundation for our words in our actions. This witness is shared in story, in our sermons imagining and creating a world in which faithful discipleship is a vibrant alternative to the depression and anxiety of the culture and in the church becoming a factory of hope and possibility. That, I hope, is the case successfully made in the preceding chapters. Now what? For that I have suggestions, not commandments, for preaching in an age of alternative facts.

EMBRACE VULNERABILITY

Educator Parker Palmer and social work professor and self-proclaimed "shame researcher" Brené Brown have done more than anyone I know to educate us on the pitfalls of using shame as parents, employers, teachers, and, by extension, preachers to motivate—or should we say manipulate—children, employees, students, and parishioners into preferred behaviors, actions, and attitudes.[1] It happens all too often, and when it happens in the pulpit the result is predictably negative. It is hard to inspire listeners to do much that is good by making them feel bad about themselves.

Palmer and Brown suggest a very different and, I would say, more Christlike path by inviting us to acknowledge our own struggles and weakness, name them, and when appropriate connect to our listeners through them. Brown writes:

> Vulnerability isn't good or bad: It's not what we call a dark emotion, nor is it always a light, positive experience. Vulnerability is the core of all emotions and feelings. To feel is to be vulnerable. To believe vulnerability is weakness is to believe that feeling is weakness. To foreclose on our emotional life out of a fear that the costs will be too high is to walk away from the very thing that gives purpose and meaning to living.
>
> Our rejection of vulnerability often stems from our associating it with dark emotions like fear, shame, grief, sadness and disappointment—emotions that we don't want to discuss, even when they profoundly affect the way we live, love, work, and even lead....Vulnerability is the birthplace of love, belonging, joy, courage, empathy, and creativity. It is the source of hope, empathy, accountability, and authenticity. If we want greater clarity in our purpose or deeper and more meaningful spiritual lives, vulnerability is the path.[2]

The listeners know we are not perfect, so there is little use in pretending otherwise. This does not mean we proclaim our failings, confess our faults, and use the pulpit as a place to work on our issues. But we do not ignore them, and when we can, we share what we have learned by acknowledging and embracing our vulnerability. What this should lead to is an appropriate humility, in our approach to and interpretation of scripture, in our reading of history and tradition, and in how we share our own stumbling efforts to practice the discipleship of righteousness. Palmer talks about teaching in a way that is filled with implications for preachers:

> I am painfully aware of the times in my own teaching when I lose touch with my inner teacher and therefore with my own authority. In those times I try to gain power by barricading myself behind the podium and my status while wielding the threat of grades. But when my teaching is authorized by the teacher within me, I need neither weapons nor armor to teach.
>
> Authority comes as I reclaim my identity and integrity, remembering my selfhood and my sense of vocation. Then teaching can come from the depths of my own truth—and the truth that is within my students as a chance to respond in kind.[3]

Replace preach/preacher for teach/teacher, pulpit for podium, and so on, and he is talking about us. Our authority comes from the Spirit of Christ within us, and when we embrace our vulnerability before God and the faithful, we discover that perhaps we are not without authority, that it is just in very different form than we thought when we first pursued the call to preach.

Embracing vulnerability means accepting our limitations, not ignoring them, and taking the great risk of preaching from the heart about things we, and likely our listeners, care about deeply. But we do not do this in constant acts of self-confession and disclosure. If the only way one can imagine talking about an issue is by talking about oneself, there is a great possibility that the preacher is the only one for whom it is an issue, and we will be talking to ourselves. All of us preach to ourselves from time to time, but that is not what embracing vulnerability means. There are more ways to take risks than saying, "Let me tell you what happened to me."

In *The Preaching of Jesus* I argued that among the characteristics of the preaching attributed to Jesus was the occasional, almost reluctant, use of the first-person singular. Of course I was here talking about the Synoptic Gospels, and not the Fourth Gospel, filled as it is with "I am" statements by Jesus. Rather than proclaiming himself Jesus, he proclaims the God's kingdom (heaven in Matthew); and when he does refer to himself, it is usually in the third person, the Son of Man. This is most dramatic in the Gospel of Mark, where there are no first-person singular references until Jesus appears before the council after his arrest and the high priest asks if he is "the Christ, the Son of the blessed one" and Jesus responds, "I am" (*egō eimi;* Mark 14:61-62). What I suggested in the book is that we follow the example of Jesus and be restrained in our use of the first-person singular in our own preaching. My argument was not just about imitation but that preachers should not squander the power of the first-person singular by using it each week. Used carefully and intentionally as testimony, the first-person singular has great rhetorical power. But not when it is used in every sermon. Use the first-person singular occasionally in your preaching so that you preserve its rhetorical power.

In part the vulnerability Palmer and Brown encourage is attitudinal, not rhetorical. No one likes a know-it-all or someone who gives the impression, as Dr. Craddock often put it, that "he has walked all the way around God and taken pictures." How can we speak of holy things with anything other than humility? If we allow this appropriate humility to shape our outlook we are much more likely to seek to persuade than prove, to invite rather than convince, and to walk alongside rather than point the way. In this season companions are needed, not guides.

All of this does fit under what Aristotle called *ethos* in his *"Art" of Rhetoric.*[4] The preacher must appear confident, but not overly so, comfortable in the role and approachable, as someone with whom the listener would enjoy sharing coffee and conversation. Vulnerability, Brown argues, is a gift because it allows us to connect with the vulnerabilities of others and allows others to see that we too have more than a few foibles of our own. Embracing our vulnerability helps us communicate authentically, inviting not demanding, seeking not to prove ourselves right and all who see things differently wrong, but showing that we are open to seeing how our listeners make a world and are willing to walk with them even as we show them how they might experience the world in faith.

BE VERY INVOLVED

Do you remember the "Emergent Church"? It turns out it was largely a publishing phenomenon, never much of an ecclesial reality, although Fresh Expressions in the United Kingdom has some life in it.[5] There was little discussion of preaching during the decade when we thought we were emerging, because as the culture was understood through emergent lenses preaching was a problem. Looking back one sees that it was the same problem addressed in *As One without Authority*, but the idea of one person talking while everyone else listens and ponders was by definition anti-emergent. Engagement, participation, de-centralization, and the deconstruction of hierarchies were central to the emergent vision. It sounded good but lacked the structures, resources, and skills needed for wide implementation. Ironically what the emergent church needed to succeed it refused in principle.

However, among the scattered remnants of the emergent vision are ideas worth remembering and, in some cases, putting into practice. One of these was the result of looking around the church and realizing that a lot of folk were gone and they were not coming back. It is a problem that has only intensified, and the continued decline has lent itself to a variety of survival strategies often geared toward finding a way for a church to afford full-time pastoral leadership. One of the most popular attempts is to yoke parishes so that two or three or more small congregations share the cost of ordained leadership. Yoking or uniting parishes has never been successful in the long term. Studies indicated that when multiple parishes were merged or yoked they would shrink to the size of the smaller of the two, three, or four, rather than grow to the size of the parish with the largest attendance. There is a more compelling reason to look for another solution: we are more likely to find a way forward by asking the pastoral leader to be deeply involved in the community of which the church is a part, the opposite of what is possible in a yoked ministry of multiple communities.

The model is an old one, but it is also the model for many successful church plants. When there is no building to meet in (and pay for and take care of), the pastoral leader focuses on the people in the neighborhood, and the life of the community of which they are all a part. Rather than inviting people to come to Sunday worship or, worse, waiting in the hope that they might come because the sign says "All are welcome!" the pastor or priest goes to them. And does what? Invite them to Sunday worship? Eventually, but not at first; at first we are simply getting acquainted and trying to understand what makes the community tick. The percentage and the source are disputed, but in my recollection it goes, "Ninety percent of success is just showing up." The preacher has to show up. Showing up shows that the preacher cares about the community and the people in it, not as a potential source of church members, but as neighbors and friends. Showing up allows the preacher to be involved in something other than church, inherently valuable for preaching but also as the way to get to know the concerns and challenges of the community. Showing up provides a way for people to get to know the preacher as something other than the professional religious person.

I doubt that in theory few will disagree that there is some wisdom in this suggestion. But most will have already determined that being very involved in the community is not possible in their situation. They will point out how time-intensive the practice would be. They will maintain that in this day members of the community will distrust an outsider and never let her or him "in." (Quote from a parishioner two years into a new ministry: "Of course you do not feel like you belong here. Your grandparents were not born here.") And if being honest, the preacher will admit that she or he is not cut out for such an approach and that in fact the idea terrifies her or him.

A few will try it, or at least will adapt the idea of being very involved in the community to the extent personality makes possible. As noted in an earlier chapter, most of us are much more comfortable talking to the altar guild than to strangers. But you may have this already going for you: you survived CPE (Clinical Pastoral Education), spending a summer or other season in ministry at a hospital or similar setting where everybody was a stranger and you were their chaplain. If it is in your background, draw on this experience. If not, remember that the quotation about success was about "just showing up," not about what you do or say after you get there.

Start where you are least uncomfortable, such as a community meeting, a coffee shop, or a ball game. It doesn't matter where, but what matters is to show up and to leave any agenda at home. You are not there to do something; you are there for the sake of being there. Then talk to people, not asking if they "go to church" or "have accepted Jesus Christ as their Lord and Savior." Talk about the meeting, the coffee, or the game.

And then go back, attend something else, maybe join something such as a choir, a team, or a civic association, not to troll for members, but to be a part of the community. Along the way you will learn some of the what and how to preach in this community, learning their questions and their challenges, their hopes and possibilities. All this can be done with or without a building, in a church start or as part of a parish renewal. The important thing is to be very involved, to be known as one of them, as a part of the town or village or neighborhood. We used to talk of this as relational evangelism, and when we did so it was something for the laity. Oddly the laity are naturally a part of the community; it is the clergy who are the outsiders. It is the preacher who needs to be very involved.

This way forward involves a redefinition of the place of ordained pastoral leadership, a different kind of involvement. With a different focus. Outward. It is risky, I suppose, but in times like these I am reminded of something (else) Fred Craddock was fond of saying: the question is not whether the church is dying, but whether it is giving its life for the world.

STICK TO THE FACTS

In an age of alternative facts it does appear most everyone is entitled to their own facts. At least many people speak and act as if they are. Faithful preachers do not have this luxury either. As tempting as it may be to appease and mollify by suggesting that we should just agree to disagree, preachers have to stand for something. They have to stand for the truth, and one of the ways they do that is by sticking to the facts.

Wait, the careful reader says, I thought you argued in the first chapter that we cannot get bogged down in arguments about data. Were you counting on us to forget a few chapters later? Fair point, and no, I hope you will remember the argument of the book from beginning to end. And the argument here is that you stick to the facts, not to the truth as expressed in oft-disputed data, but the facts that are indisputable. Not opinions; facts. Which is not saying that we abandon a focus on truth as righteousness or begin to emphasize faith as attitude and opinion rather than something that is a living, daily practice. Still, there is a difference between what we stand on and insist on and what we hope for, and there is no getting from the one to the other without commitment and tenacity, the first of these familiar in every church and the second almost never mentioned. Tenacity.

God being good all the time, my reading led me to this astonishing quote from a writer I do not recall encountering before:

> Let us never forget that it was the best and the brightest who engineered the debacle of the Vietnam War. But I take hope in every politician or economist's statement that Americans aren't buying enough; in every student's reference to "sustainability" and "mindfulness," terms that weren't in my college vocabulary; in the expansion of the concept and increasing use of queer, founded in a shared resistance to the dominant model, the glorification of greed. I have faith in the capacity of the truth, *if brought to light and given time*, to win its cause; the capacity of love to win its cause.[6]

"I have faith in the capacity of truth, *if brought to light and given time*, to win its cause." What a compelling way to understand the preaching task, to bring to light and give time to the truth. And to do this we must stick to the facts, from two times two is four to the world is round and revolves around the sun to our planet is warming and there are some practical things we can do about that if we want to. American democracy is founded on three equal branches of government, and no one is above the law. Equality has meaning, and inequality has consequences. The prophet Jesus and his prophetic forebears had some challenging things to say about inequality and what a faithful response before God looks like, well summarized by the Apostle Paul in the Letter to the Romans: "owe no one anything, except to love one another" (13:8). Our challenge as preachers is to show, Sunday after Sunday, what a faithful response to the love of God can look like, bringing the truth of Christ to light over time.

So stick to your beliefs, stick to what you know, and stick to the facts. Your beliefs, commitments, and understanding of the facts must be open to challenge and dialogue, but you do not abandon them in order to curry favor. Ever.

We also have to reject the kind of false equivalences so pronounced in our public discourse.

Everyone is doing it.
They are all corrupt.
What difference does it make?

It makes all the difference in the world. We have been hearing a lot about "what about-ism" in this age. What about so-and-so? They are doing the same thing, something worse, and so on. What about-ism was born in a spirit of a "nothing to see here," "look, over there!" and "don't look behind the curtain" relativism that hopes the reader/listener/observer cannot tell the difference between false equivalences. It assumes we are stupid or are so fully brainwashed that we can no longer think for ourselves.

To a certain extent media coverage over the years has conditioned us to think creating such equivalences is central to unbiased reporting, so it must be central to unbiased preaching. I have no idea what unbiased preaching is, though, so this is not my problem. All preaching worth hearing is biased, that is, it comes from someone with a set of commitments, priorities, and an understanding of what faithful discipleship looks like. It reads scripture out of those commitments and does not say, "Sixteen hundred years ago it was commonly held that the Apostle Paul wrote the Letter to the Hebrews, so let's see what happens if we read it that way today." Let alone, "Hal Lindsey and the Left Behind folk wrote extensively on the book of Revelation, so it is only fair to follow their lead and read apocalyptic literature as if it made no sense whatsoever for almost two thousand years, but now we have the keys to unlock its mysteries: it is all about oil, Russians, and a red heifer." If you believe that, if you want to read scripture that way, have at it. But all that means is that your biases are different than mine, not that you do not have any.

No, leave false equivalencies to newscasters and prognosticators. Stand for what you believe and stick to the facts because you know it is the truth that sets us free.

REMEMBER THAT TRUTH IS RIGHTEOUSNESS

Truth. There it is again. For all the beating it has taken this millennium it will not go away. I will for the last time make the argument that for preachers truth is not primarily about data but about righteousness. Our proclamation is inextricably bound up in our faith, and that faith is a series of practices, not a set of beliefs. Recall where we started, "Just because you are angry it doesn't mean you are a prophet." What does make you a prophet? Two words: zeal and righteousness. Zeal is our passion, our commitment, and our energy for the work and witness of faith. Righteousness is our way.

In one of Jesus's many ironic sayings he instructed the crowds regarding the scribes and Pharisees, "Therefore, you must take care to do everything they say. But don't do what they do" (Matt 23:3). I suppose this is one of the ways to realize that pastors, priests, and preachers are not the contemporary answer to biblical scribes and Pharisees, because everybody is looking at what we do to evaluate whether our words have merit. And as much as preaching professors loathe the (in)famous St. Francis quote about proclaiming the gospel, "If necessary, use words," if we have not laid a foundation in our actions, our words are worse than meaningless; they are hypocritical, and that is the ultimate put-down these days.

Righteousness is a catch-all term for the practices we also gather under the term *discipleship*. It has a slightly more pious ring to it, and that's okay. To live as a *tsadiq* is to live according to the commandments, and their interpretation, within Judaism. So we have to be careful about cultural misappropriation. To live righteously is not creed-specific, and from the perspective of the Christian confession it brings *dikaiosunē*, with its more juridical emphasis, into the conversation. We are righteous by faith so that we may live righteously.

Faithful preaching is a part of the right practice of ministry. What this looks like is as clear as it is challenging: focusing on the biblical text and its faithful exposition; deeply and persistently listening to the needs, questions, and hopes of the listeners as they hear and reflect on these texts; persistently using figurative material to help the listeners make connections and applications of the texts to their own spiritual practice, all done in prayerful confidence under the guidance of the Holy Spirit. This is where and how we proclaim the truth of the gospel.

NEVER PREACH AROUND AN ISSUE

Every time we find ourselves asking how so-and-so might react to something we are considering including in a sermon we are in danger of the most insidious censorship of all, self-censorship. Here we have to stop, take stock, say our prayers, and honestly ask what we think is at stake.

I am guided here not by a *homiletician* but by a *physician* turned leadership expert, Ron Heifetz. From *Leadership without Easy Answers* to *The Practice of Adaptive Leadership*, Heifetz has written and lectured for a generation from his position at the Harvard Kennedy School on how to guide individuals and institutions in confronting problems everyone wishes would just go away.[7] He distinguishes adaptive problems from technical problems, pointing out that while one might wish for the quick fix of a technical solution ("If we hire the right young person our youth group will rebound!"), most problems come from complex and multiple sources, involve a variety of stakeholders with differing priorities, and will steadfastly resist simple answers.

Preaching, Sunday after Sunday, is very much one of the "tools and tactics for changing your organization and the world," to quote the subtitle of *The Practice of Adaptive Leadership*. But it is not the one-off of the angry prophet railing against the godless. It is the faithful practice of "gradually turning up the heat" (*Leadership without Easy Answers*), not on the frogs in the kettle, but on those who hope things will magically improve. Our preaching must adjust the discomfort with the status quo in ways that do not put people off or cause them to shut down but in ways that allow them to process their own concerns and hopes until they, or enough of them, are ready for change. That may not sound prophetic, but it is faithful. And much more likely to result in positive change.

One cannot reduce twenty-five years of Heifetz into a couple of paragraphs. What he importantly invites us to do is to think about the longer trajectory of our preaching and, if we are privileged to be part of a preaching team, regularly sharing the same pulpit with others on staff, our collective impact over time. Meaningful change rarely comes in a moment, even when looking back one sees pivotal points along the way. Preachers cannot shape a congregational hermeneutic by one sermon on the historicity of Job and Jonah. Nor can we do so by accepting as inevitable a hermeneutic that does not allow discussion of Job and Jonah's timelessness. We chip away at what we believe is inadequate, hermeneutically, ethically, and so on, and lay a foundation for more faithful responses. The preacher who talks about stewardship once a year has the pledges to show for it. Nobody wants to talk about money all the time. Except Jesus. Oh.

This digression to Heifetz is to bolster the argument that we never preach around an issue, but that does not mean we preach through it on one occasion and say, "There. I've told 'em. Now it's up to them." If the goal—whether it be stewardship, use of church property, a pending decision of the town council or school board, a change in liturgy or hymnody, the addition of a new worship service, the makeup of the church board, session, vestry, and so on, to better reflect the diversity of the membership, whatever it is—is worth preaching about once, it is worth preaching about over time. We address issues patiently, faithfully, and sometimes indirectly, using story and metaphor to do the hard work of changing hearts and minds. That is not avoidance, but it is also not confrontation, neither of which should describe our preaching.

There is a big assumption here that must be considered: good preaching, while it happens one Sunday at a time, must be planned out over a much longer horizon. Rare is the preacher who asks, "What do I hope will happen because of my preaching this year?" The tyranny of Sunday is thought to prevent that. Lectionary preachers also often feel that their only responsibility is the readings for this week. At the same time they express jealousy at their colleagues' freedom to have a sermon series because they do not use the lectionary. Planning makes it possible for lectionary preachers to do topical series, and for any preacher to take the long view. Stewardship, of finances and creation, is best explored over time as part of persistent reflection on discipleship. Encouraging social, civic, and political engagement does not successfully happen in a single sermon illustration but in a regular inclusion of the topic, faithfully and positively depicted in stories and examples, over a month of Sundays.

Preachers rarely confront issues and topics head on without unintended consequences that do more damage than the confrontation did good. But this does not mean such issues and topics are ignored. Instead we plan to patiently and persistently show a faithful response in sermon after sermon, slowly working our way through resistance to an openness to change. It happens but not by accident.

TELL BETTER STORIES

We have previously discussed the gap between theory and practice on the use of illustrative material in preaching, so that even the theorists questioning the role of story and narrative in preaching use stories to make their point. What has not changed as far as most preachers can tell is the love of most of their listeners for good stories. This shifts the question in a helpful direction: what constitutes a good story?

Start with the origin of the story. How did it come to be a candidate for this sermon on this occasion in the first place? Stories whose origin is some other sermon, for some other occasion and set of texts, that struck the preacher in a way that might be summarized as, "That's good; I'm going to use that," are always suspect. Especially when the story appears at the top of the page, before the readings, before the sketch of possible moves driving the sermon. Nothing is never and nothing is always in preaching (don't sing!), but a sermon whose preparation begins with a story and is crafted around the story rather than around the text, the listeners, and the answer to the homiletical question is a problem waiting to happen. One never wants to hear, "The best sermon you ever preached was about the time your hair caught on fire!" Stories find their way into our sermons, but they are not the focus, let alone the origin, of our sermons.

Does the story fit in the sermon, both in the move of which it is a part and the sermon as a whole? Sermons have themes and tones, and the illustrative material should be a part of it, not apart from it. Everyone loves to laugh; not every homiletical occasion calls for laughter. Fit is also a matter of scope and length. If, as Buttrick (and Brosend) maintain, a move is a two-and-a-half- to four-minute unit of discourse, which makes a theological, biblical, ethical, or other claim, and develops and illustrates the claim before reiterating it and transitioning to the next claim, the story used to develop the claim cannot be five minutes long.[8] Stories must not overwhelm our sermons but enhance their impact and connection.

Illustrative material must be appropriate to a sermon's claim on the listener. One does not illustrate the love of God carelessly. Everybody loves puppies. Does that make our love for a puppy a fitting comparison for God's love of the world? What analogies might one use for the mystery of the Holy Trinity? Shamrocks? Ice/water/steam? What is appropriate for a children's story is not necessarily suitable for a sermon.

(Pet peeve: the temptation and Transfiguration of Jesus lead to sermons about how we too are tempted and might be transformed. Really? Because without the forty days of fasting and talking to Satan, or unless the listener is going to become transcendently white and gets to talk to Moses and Elijah, my guess is those two stories are about Jesus, not us. End of digression.)

So weigh in a delicate balance whether the story or comparison you think will help the listeners understand the theological claim is adequate for the majesty of the claim the preacher wants to make. Otherwise the atonement becomes a cancelled library fine (it has happened).

This may seem obvious, but good stories work. Not that they evoke laughter or tears or nods of recognition, though they might. Good stories work to move the sermon forward; they work homiletically. One of the problems with illustrative material is that it has a life of its own. There is no guarantee the listeners will make the connection with the claim the preacher has in mind. An effective story about forgiveness invites the listener to reflect on moments of forgiveness, or the lack of them, in their own lives, not to question the behavior or motivations of the characters in the story. Or worse, those of the speaker.

One of the challenges for all preachers is to work far enough in advance to have time to edit, to ask among other things, "Does this story do what I need it to do homiletically?"

The argument from indirection asks us to use illustrative material to explore topics nonconfrontationally, to make our claims a source of dialogue, not demand. They also allow the preacher to more effectively show what it looks like to live rightly as disciples of

Jesus Christ, in ways that are recognizable to the listeners. That is, we need to tell stories about people that look like our listeners and not always look like the saints and heroes of the tradition. This does not mean we do not talk about biblical characters, but we should talk about Abraham and Sarah like they are standing in front of us in the checkout line at the grocery store, not as remote and distant figures.

This adds a last suggestion: we should make our stories diverse and aspirational. Most storytellers have a default setting; usually their characters look more like them, *their* family, and *their* friends, than anyone else. Preachers need to tell stories about people who look like their listeners, not themselves, and who also look like the people they hope will one day be listening to their sermons. If every family has two kids who always come home for the holidays, if every person has struggles at work and never struggles to find work, if the leaders are male and the immigrants are always on the margin for us to help should we choose to, our stories are about caricatures, not characters.

Where will you find these stories? That is discussed in *The Homiletical Question* in some detail, but it comes down to this: have a life, and learn how to make stuff up. Preachers are bad at the former, and the latter sounds awfully suspicious in an age of alternative facts, but both are necessary.

YOU STILL HAVE TO ASK THE HOMILETICAL QUESTION

I apologize for returning time and again to previously published work. And God knows my method need not be your method, but you do have to have a method, no matter whose you have adapted for your own needs. The critical thing is the discipline. That and the refusal to give into the temptation that preaching in an age of alternative facts is an excuse for anything other than homiletical discipline. On the contrary, it makes that discipline all the more important.

When passion and frustration are running high, homiletical discipline keeps us grounded. When words threaten to escape the preacher's lips before planning, prayer, and reflection, method keeps us in check. By asking, "What does the Holy Spirit want the people of God to hear from these texts on this occasion?" (or some variation), we keep ourselves and our task honest. Listeners and texts remain front and center, until an occasion in the life of the church, community, nation, or world overwhelms the lectionary or our preaching calendar and we must address it directly and fully. Even then, though, we must apply the method we would use on the thirty-eleventh Sunday after whenever, and not begin our preparations with, "I've got to talk about this, no matter what." No matter what? I always worry about preachers who say that or who say, "I always…" Nothing is never and nothing is always in preaching, but homiletical discipline is especially helpful when we are most likely to set it aside in times of passion.

ASK FOR HELP

No preacher is an island, John Donne might have written but did not. But all too often you could not tell on Sunday morning. Part of this is for very good reason—that is, the desire to avoid plagiarism. It may also be because the preacher is committed to offering a sermon that is only her best efforts, under the guidance and inspiration of the Holy Spirit, in response to the biblical texts for the day and the needs, hopes, and questions of her listeners.

This is wonderful until we get stuck. Stuck happens in two main fashions, within a single sermon or in a rut of preaching Sunday after Sunday (after Sunday). Fortunately, while ruts happen they need not be disabling. We preach in community, and we are a part of a community of preachers, if we are intentional about it. We have to be willing to ask for help. Doing so is not a sign of weakness. Quite the contrary; asking for help is a sign of a confident preacher who wants to grow.

When we are stuck on one particular sermon the need to reach out is immediate, be it to a colleague in the church, a family member, or a parishioner. The only thing between us and the help we need is pride. "Hey, have you got a minute? I am having a problem with Sunday's sermon and it would be really helpful to talk it through if you would be willing to listen." Who would say no to that? God, for one, is listening, and talking out loud can be an excellent way to hear where the problem might be. But a former seminary classmate, the preacher across town, even—and this may surprise you—your former preaching professor are among those who would be happy to listen if you are willing to reach out. In this age of alternative facts, when biblical texts and current events have a habit of smashing into each other in ways that turn the nave into a nuclear reactor, such reaching out is also an important check on our outrage and anger. Maybe this is the Sunday to tell it like it is. But maybe the shape of this sermon is not the best way to do that. If you have any doubt ask for help.

The other rut is more insidious, which makes it all the more unlikely we will ask for help. And all the more important that we do so. No preacher is an island, entire unto herself. "We were made for community" is a refrain often found in our sermons. So if we truly believe in laying a foundation for our words in our actions, why not in our preaching preparations? Why not be part of a community of preachers? This can be easy in a large parish with three or more preachers regularly sharing the pulpit, although it is rare and is entirely up to the senior preacher on staff. It is also surprisingly possible in other settings, if you are willing to be the catalyst. The Religion Division of the Lilly Endowment, Inc., has even been willing to help make it happen through the Pastoral Excellence Network program at the Christian Theological Seminary in Indianapolis.[9]

The key, the Rev. Sharon Hiers found in her Doctor of Ministry in Preaching project, is found not in lectionary study groups but in sermon evaluation groups, in which preachers watch or listen to each other's sermons and gather periodically for discussion and feedback, before looking ahead to the texts coming up.[10] It may sound like seminary preaching class but without the professor, and to a certain extent it is because it allows preachers to get the critical feedback they need to grow, not just, "Nice sermon, pastor," on Sunday.

SPEAK FROM YOUR HEAD, NOT JUST YOUR HEART

Sometimes it is time, and this week is it. Not because you have had it up to here or there was a decision or action in the political arena that must be addressed. In this climate that happens every week, even every day. But some convergence of text(s) and occasion has brought matters to a moment when you, dear preacher, have decided to weigh in. Big time. If you are preacher who is paying attention, cares about the kingdom, the church, and your listeners, and cares about the community, nation, and world, it will happen.

And when it is time I ask one big favor: use your head, not just your heart. You may lead with your heart. You may care so passionately you have no choice. But energy, excitement, and enthusiasm, not to mention outrage, umbrage, and frustration, will only get you so far. If you are to be persuasive, you have to keep your head and use your head.

CONCLUSION

Sermons should rarely come full circle, although nothing is never and nothing is always in preaching. This is a book not a sermon, although God knows I have been preaching along the way, so allow me to review.

- You may be angry, but that does not make you a prophet. The last thing in the world I want to take away is a preacher's passion, but when that passion flashes out in a burst of anger, or slides into snarky disparagement of difference, it is a problem. Remember that the prophets were not sent simply to denounce the people but to bring them home to God.

- Do you want to listen as much as you want to be heard? In my seminary, the students go to chapel and listen to sermons for three semesters before they take their turn in the pulpit. The week before they present their first sermon, students receive a message that says, among other things, "If you have been waiting three semesters to finally have your chance to straighten everyone out, wait longer." Every preacher has something she or he is dying to say. But is that what God wants those gathered to hear?

- They know how you voted. Do they know how much you care about them, about the community? This will not be a surprise: McGovern, Carter, Carter, Mondale,

Dukakis, Clinton, Clinton, Gore, Kerry, Obama, Obama, Clinton. If you had any doubt you now know that the author votes like a "yellow dog Democrat," i.e., someone who would vote for a yellow dog before they would vote for a Republican. After a few weeks, anyone listening to our sermons probably knows how we voted. This only matters if they do not know of your love for the Lord, the church, and for them, and if they are not learning that you vote the way you do because your faith has led you to do so.

- Have you laid a foundation for your words in your deeds and actions? Talk is still cheap unless it is surrounded by a great cloud of witnesses. This is why a preacher can talk about things, and talk about them in ways she would never dare to in year one. After a few years as in a particular corner of the kingdom, pastors lay the foundation as teachers, through pastoral care, and in our involvement with causes we champion.

- You must still ask the homiletical question: what does the Holy Spirit want the people of God to hear from these texts on this occasion? As much as I like my method, I am more concerned that you have the discipline to follow *a* method in this homiletical season. The more passionate we are about a passage or a topic, the more important this is. We do not want to begin our preparation with, "What do I want to talk about on Sunday?" We absolutely do not want to begin with, "This is the week I finally tell them what I really think!"

- When the time comes, speak your mind, not just your heart. Do not make the mistake of thinking that others care about something as much as you do. Do not make the mistake of thinking that caring passionately about an issue will automatically translate into preaching convincingly about it. We have to persuade, and that means making the case, not hoping that our passion will do it for us.

WE HOLD THESE TRUTHS TO BE SELF-EVIDENT

I have struggled throughout this book to talk about *truth* in an age of alternative facts, as if truth were something elusive, or like beauty, merely in the eye of the beholder. Why the struggle? Dumbfounded incredulity, I suppose. Because, or so I thought, it is one thing to argue about the situational nature of truth in debates about gender and race, to admit that history is open to interpretation, as is scripture. But it seems quite another to dispute the veracity of empirical data, visual evidence, the reliability of audio and videotape, and the testimony of experts in his or her field. Yet this is where we are. Everything is partisan, and it will be for the foreseeable future. And then there is this: "We hold these truths to be self-evident, that all men are created equal, that they are endowed by their Creator with certain unalienable rights, that among these are life, liberty, and the pursuit of happiness."

We now live and preach in a time when the almost 250-year-old document upon which our nation was launched into the world begins with words that are thoroughly contested and denied. Not that "all men" should be read like the Greek *anthrōpos* upon which it was likely based, and so "all people" or simply "all." Nor that this "all" includes not just those free born, land-holding people already on these shores but is now understood to mean what it says, everybody.

No, such semantic obscurities are not the problem. The problem is that we no longer hold these or any truths to be self-evident. In an age of alternative facts even the Declaration of Independence is a partisan document, its self-evident truths disputed and denied.

This is the season in which we now preach. It is not the only such season in our nation's history, but the impact and intensification of twenty-four-hour news and the amplification of social media have created a homiletical challenge without precedent. Add to this the church's own divisions and decline and the problem seems intractable. It is not.

I have argued that the way forward for preachers is to engage the conflicts, issues, and divides found at almost every level of society, not least including our churches, but to do so indirectly. The battle for truth has been lost, epistemologically at least, and there is no point in arguing on that front. But the battle is not the war. In part this is because the truth in view is more like Colbert's "truthiness" than those truths deemed as *self-evident* to our nation's founders. More important, all is not lost because the foundation of the truth in our sermons is much older than the Declaration of Independence. It is biblical. Grounded as we are in biblical truth, with its emphasis on righteousness as the way of discipleship, we follow and proclaim the One who is way and truth and life. We do not relativize our biblical exegesis, our theological reflection, or our interpretation of the contemporary situation to please or pander. We stick to the facts, do not propose false equivalences, and do not disseminate things we know are not true for rhetorical advantage. We do not bear false witness.

Good sermons, in every age, have spoken "truth to power." That cannot stop because truth is now partisan and contested. It was never going to make preachers popular, and it will not now. The balancing act for preachers is to remain popular enough to keep our jobs while telling people some things they might rather not hear.

Years ago—for some of us, quite a few years ago—we responded to an urging, an invitation, a call. We studied and trained, sought endorsement, and began to think of ourselves as a preacher. We did all this because we knew that we could make a difference. That has not changed. Pray to God you will make all the difference you can.

So how can they call on someone they don't have faith in?

And how can they have faith in someone they haven't heard of?

And how can they hear without a preacher?

And how can they preach unless they are sent? "As it is written, *How beautiful are the feet of those who announce the good news*" (Rom 10:15).

NOTES

INTRODUCTION

1. Ben Zimmer, "Truthiness," *The New York Times*, October 17, 2010, Sunday Magazine, MM22.

2. I intentionally avoided quotation marks around coined or disputed words and phrases. There are simply too many of them.

3. Bryan Stephenson, *Just Mercy: A Story of Justice and Redemption* (New York: Spiegel & Grau, 2015).

4. William Brosend, "The Letter of Jude: A Rhetoric of Excess or an Excess of Rhetoric?" *Interpretation: A Journal of Bible and Theology*, volume 60. no. 3, July 2006, 292-305.

5. Eugene Lowry, *The Homiletical Plot: The Sermon as Narrative Art Form* (Louisville: Westminster John Knox Press, 2001).

6. William Brosend, *The Preaching of Jesus: Gospel Proclamation Then and Now* (Louisville: Westminster John Knox Press, 2010).

1. TRUTH

1. Charles Taylor, *A Secular Age* (Cambridge: Belknap Press, 2007).

2. "Homiletical" ethos will be discussed in chapter 2.

2. LISTENING

1. Fred B. Craddock, *As One without Authority* (Nashville: Abingdon Press, 1971) and *Overhearing the Gospel* (Nashville: Abingdon Press, 1978).

2. William Brosend, *The Preaching of Jesus: Gospel Proclamation Then and Now* (Louisville: Westminster John Knox Press 2010), Ch. 3.

3. Thomas G. Long, "Taking the Listeners Seriously in Biblical Interpretation" in *The Folly of Preaching*, ed. Michael P. Knowles (Grand Rapids, MI: Eerdmans, 2007), 73.

4. Ibid., 73–74.

3. BEARING WITNESS

1. Mahatma Gandhi, *All Men Are Brothers: Autobiographical Impressions* (Paris: UNESCO, 1958), 99.

2. William Brosend, *James and Jude*, New Cambridge Bible Commentary (Cambridge: Cambridge University Press, 2004).

3. *The Book of Common Prayer*, 305.

4. My New Testament colleague and friend Amy-Jill Levine has done much to remind us that preachers continue to bear false witness against Judaism in the depiction of Judaism in sermons. Despite two generations of scholarship teaching us that much of what we learned in Sunday school about Jews in the Second Temple period is not true, preachers perpetuate negative stereotypes by denigrating Judaism in contrast with their depictions of Jesus and Paul, as if Jesus and Paul were not themselves Jews. Here is the simple rule in my classroom: You do not have to make Jews look bad in order to make Jesus look good. Jesus looks good all by himself. Among Dr. Levine's many helpful works I especially recommend *The Jewish Annotated New Testament* (New York: Oxford University Press, 2017), which Dr. Levine co-edited.

4. HOW

1. Thomas G. Long, *The Witness of Preaching*, 3rd ed. (Louisville: Westminster John Knox Press, 2016).

2. William Brosend, *The Homiletical Question: An Introduction to Liturgical Preaching* (Eugene, OR: Cascade Books, 2017).

3. Edward Farley, "Interpreting Situations: An Essay in Practical Theology" reprinted in *Formation and Reflection: The Promise of Practical Theology*, ed. Lewis Mudge and James Poling (Philadelphia: Fortress Press, 1987), 1–26.

4. Fred Craddock, *Overhearing the Gospel* (Nashville: Abingdon Press, 1978).

5. The evidence from the rabbis is precisely that, evidence from the rabbinic, not from the Second Temple period. Moreover, it was compiled two centuries after the Gospels. While the stories attributed to the rabbis are wonderful in their own right, they differ significantly from the parables of Jesus. See my *Conversations with Scripture: The Parables* (Harrisburg, PA: Morehouse Publishing, 2006).

6. William Brosend, *The Preaching of Jesus* (Louisville: Westminster John Knox Press, 2010).

7. Marcus Borg and John Dominic Crossan, *The Last Week: What the Gospels Really Teach Us about Jesus's Final Days in Jerusalem* (San Francisco: Harper One, 2007).

8. You will have to trust me here. I wanted to show you how easy it is to craft a story to advance the claim of a sermon. This morning I read an essay in *The New Yorker* magazine (January 1, 2018, pp. 63–65), "A Symphony on Skid Row" by Alex Ross, about members of the Los Angeles Philharmonic who are reaching out to the homeless in downtown LA. Character, plot, and conclusion: instant illustration.

9. Malcolm Gladwell, "The 10,000 Hour Rule" in *Outliers: The Story of Success* (New York: Little, Brown and Company, 2008), 35–68.

10. *Book of Common Prayer*, 101.

11. Ibid, 362.

5. SOME SUGGESTIONS

1. See especially Parker Palmer, *The Courage to Teach* (San Francisco: Josey-Bass, 2007) and Brené Brown, *Daring Greatly: How the Courage to Be Vulnerable Transforms the Way We Live, Love, Parent and Lead* (New York: Avery, 2012).

2. Brown, *Daring Greatly*, 33–34.

3. Palmer, *The Courage to Teach*, 34.

4. Aristotle, *The "Art" of Rhetoric*, trans. J. H. Freese, Loeb Classical Library (Cambridge: Harvard University Press, 1926).

5. Among many others, Diana Butler Bass, *Christianity for the Rest of Us* (San Francisco: Harper One, 2007); Phyllis Tickle, *The Great Emergence: How Christianity Is Changing and Why* (Grand Rapids: Baker Books, 2012); Tony Jones, *The New Christians: Dispatches from the Emergent Frontier* (San Francisco: Josey-Bass, 2008); and Brian McLaren, *A Generous Orthodoxy* (Grand Rapids: Youth Specialties Books, 2004).

6. Fenton Johnson, "The Future of Queer: A Manifesto," *Harper's Magazine*, January 2018, 32. Emphasis in the original.

7. Ron Heifetz, *Leadership without Easy Answers* (Cambridge, MA: Harvard University Press, 1998). Ronald Heiftetz, Alexander Grashow, Marty Linsky, *The Practice of Adaptive Leadership* (Cambridge, MA: Harvard Business Review Press, 2009). The latter is assigned reading in my Advanced Preaching course.

8. See David Buttrick, *Homiletic: Moves and Structures* (Philadelphia: Fortress Press, 1987) and William Brosend, *The Homiletical Question: An Introduction to Liturgical Preaching* (Eugene, OR: Cascade Books, 2017). Eric Hinds, in "Film Narratives in Preaching," explored the most effective length of narrative material in sermons and concluded that on most occasions the shorter version of a narrative was more effective (Doctor of Ministry in Preaching thesis, School of Theology, The University of the South, 2016).

9. To learn more about Lilly Endowment, Inc. programs for pastoral leaders, go to http://www.cpx.cts.edu/renewal.

10. Sharon Hiers, "Peer Mentoring for Preachers" (Doctor of Ministry in Preaching thesis, School of Theology, The University of the South, 2016).

CPSIA information can be obtained
at www.ICGtesting.com
Printed in the USA
LVHW05s0751200618
581297LV00001B/1/P